The One-Burner Cookbook

The One-Burner Cookbook

MARY BETH JUNG

COLLIER BOOKS
MACMILLAN PUBLISHING COMPANY
New York

Macmillan Publishing Company
866 Third Avenue, New York, N.Y. 10022
Collier Macmillan Canada, Inc.

Library of Congress Cataloging-in-Publication Data
Jung, Mary Beth.
    The one-burner cookbook.
    Includes index.
    1. Cookery.   I. Title.
TX652.J86 1986   641.5   86-5357

Macmillan books are available at special discounts for bulk purchases for
sales promotions, premiums, fund-raising, or educational use. For details
contact:
    Special Sales Director
    Macmillan Publishing Company
    866 Third Avenue
    New York, New York 10022

10 9 8 7 6 5 4 3 2 1

Printed in the United States of America

For Mom and Dad

ACKNOWLEDGMENTS

I wish to thank my mother for her loving support, helpful suggestions, and late-night proofing sessions on this book; Ceal Langer for volunteering her copyediting talents, her long days and late nights, and, most of all, her friendship; Melinda Corey and Emily Easton, associate editors at Macmillan, for their help along the way. Lastly a "thank you" to all my friends for their patience while I was totally absorbed in the writing of this book.

Contents

Introduction

Why a *one-burner* cookbook?

There are so many reasons for writing this kind of book and so many people to write it for! Primarily this book was written for:

- People who live in small apartments, studio apartments, condominiums, trailers, dorm rooms, hotel rooms, boats, cabins, summer homes, and campers.
- Single adults who are tired of fast-food restaurants.
- Retired people who live in small quarters but want home-cooked meals at home-cooked prices.
- Working parents whose quality family time is at a premium.
- Noncooks who have little desire to be gourmet cooks but simply want foolproof recipes to prepare for themselves and occasional guests.
- New graduates living on their own for the first time.
- Anyone else who wants new easy menu ideas, including the author!

Yes, I wrote this book for me! Even though I'm a home economist, I know how difficult it can be to plan meals on those busy nights after work. I hear that comment from the consumers I come in contact with daily. I also know, first hand, what it's like to prepare an entire meal in a small condominium kitchen that is not much larger than any one of my closets. You've never lived until you've prepared an entire Thanksgiving dinner for six from my well-appointed but miniature kitchen.

You can also imagine the space shock I experience every

night when I start to prepare the evening meal after spending most of the day in a glamorous test kitchen, larger than most luxury two-bedroom apartments. So, from this first-hand experience, and because of my background in the food area, I decided to share my own solutions to kitchen space problems by writing this book on *one-burner* cooking.

Besides tackling the space problem, the *one-burner* concept also seemed to offer a solution to the ever-increasing demands on my time. I decided that if I was going to enjoy eating more meals at home from my small kitchen I needed to develop real time-saving recipes for myself! So I did.

I began concocting, testing, and retesting 10- to 15-minute main dishes that tasted and looked like I'd fussed for hours. I also developed ways to prepare some of my old-fashioned and gourmet favorites and convert them to single-burner preparation. I didn't want to wash every pot in the house anymore! The more recipes I converted to a single burner, the more I was convinced that this concept was going to work.

My testing schedule detoured when my editor and I decided to try to convert some of the classic oven-baked dessert favorites to the *one-burner* concept. I stocked my pantry with butter, flour, nuts, and chocolate. I was off to the challenge of developing cakes, cookies, and brownies in a skillet.

I found upside-down cakes, Bundt cakes, and the like could be prepared in a skillet over a low heat without an oven. What fun for those who don't have an oven or those who want to bake desserts over the campfire! With these successes to my credit, I decided to test my favorites, the chocolate chip cookie and the brownie.

I tested the chocolate chip drop cookie with no success. Should I add more butter, less sugar? Nothing worked. I never saw so many burnt cookie offerings. Finally, I decided to move on to the brownie recipe. Success! I developed a chewy brownie that was delicious when baked on a single burner. I did learn that some recipes, like the chocolate chip cookie, could not be improved upon or adapted to my *one-burner* format.

Despite the demise of the *one-burner* chocolate chip cookie, I did have hundreds of successes during my testing. I began having more company to show off these new time-and-space-saving recipes in my repertoire. My guests couldn't believe that I had arrived home only 30 minutes before they rang the doorbell. Depending on the guests, I reserved the right to explain the painless preparation of my newfound *one-burner* secret (as good cooks do on occasion!). But when I did divulge my secret, no one could believe that my famous Chicken with Green Peppercorn Sauce took only 15 minutes from skillet to platter. And the best part—I had only one pan to wash!

As the book neared completion, I continued to talk to my peers about this *one-burner* concept. All of them told me that they would cook more, especially after work and for dinner parties, if preparation was hassle free, cleanup was minimal, and the result was glamorous. A tall order, but I think you'll be surprised and delighted that the recipes and menus in this book fit that bill.

From appetizer to flaming dessert, there is a menu for any occasion, for any price, and for any level of culinary expertise. As one of my friends commented, while we completed the last-minute editing, "Now I don't have any excuse. I can cook in my studio apartment, and do it with flair!"

This concept, cooking on *one burner*, is the solution for me. It helps me enjoy home-cooked meals during the week and allows me to entertain at home more, and like it! It really works!

Bon Appétit!

—*Mary Beth Jung*

The One-Burner Cookbook

1
Tricks of the Trade
Buying Equipment and Menu Planning

Have you ever said, "If I only knew some of those little organizational tricks in the kitchen, I could really get into cooking"? Well, this chapter will set the stage for all the fun that's about to begin. With a little information on how to select proper *one-burner* cookware and how to plan *one-burner* menus you'll be ready to have some fun in no time. Yes, we must eat to live, but let's have fun planning meals for one or for several, and for entertaining even if we only have small kitchens.

Read this chapter before you go on to the recipes. Evaluate your kitchen utensils and make a few purchases, if necessary. Add optional equipment as you develop your own cooking style.

The second half of this chapter deals with planning meals. This may seem less than exciting, but these classic techniques are used by good cooks and chefs the world over. Cooking is just like other disciplines; it requires organization. Cooking can be a very enjoyable solo or social activity if you're organized.

Basic Equipment Tricks for One-Burner Recipes

This is a book for the person who wants to streamline time and effort spent in the kitchen. The basic kitchen equipment needed to accomplish this end should be carefully analyzed before any purchases are made. Depending on your life-style, select only the cookware pieces you need. No matter how many you choose, be sure to buy good-to-excellent quality. You will find that in kitchenware you definitely get what you pay for. For the best day-to-day cooking results, as well as minimal replacement, invest in quality.

WHAT WILL YOU NEED?

Good news! Very little, because, undoubtedly, your kitchen is small. Choose the size pan by the size of your family or the quantity you will be cooking. I prefer buying the larger pans, because they're more versatile than smaller sizes and no harder to store or clean. It is also very common among good cooks to "cherrypick" with cookware; that is, to buy individual pieces of different types for specific needs. It is not necessary or recommended to buy entire cookware sets, especially for small kitchens. I would suggest the following equipment.

BASIC COOKWARE

> 2- or 3-quart saucepan with cover
>
> 5- to 8-quart Dutch oven with cover
>
> 9- to 12-inch skillet or frying pan with cover

OPTIONAL COOKWARE PIECES

> Square griddle   Fondue pot
>
> Wok with cover   6-inch sauté
>
>   or omelet pan

ELECTRIC OR TOP-OF-THE-RANGE COOKWARE?

Based on your particular kitchen situation, you may want to purchase skillets, frying pans, Dutch ovens, and woks in either electric or nonelectric models. If you do not have a range, want to conserve electricity, or want to increase your cooking space, the purchase of an electric cooking utensil could be advantageous. You will find the electric counterparts of these pots and pans have better temperature controls than range-top burners.

WHAT KIND OF MATERIAL SHOULD I LOOK FOR IN COOKWARE?

Generally speaking, heavy-gauge *aluminum* is the best buy for your money. It's a good conductor of heat, easy to clean, and requires little care.

Stainless steel is very attractive and can be an excellent cooking vessel if it has a core of aluminum or another good, even conductor of heat. When cooking on stainless, you must remember to use medium to low heat because it is a very rapid heat conductor, having a tendency to *"hot spot"* over high heat.

Cast iron has long been the favorite of good cooks. Its even heating and excellent browning capabilities are a real bonus for the serious cook who loves to prepare all the country stews and pot roasts with rich gravy. Cast iron does require care and special handling, but the addition of a frying pan or stew kettle might be desirable in some kitchens.

Always try to purchase the heaviest gauge cookware that you can afford. Prices will vary greatly as the quality goes up the ladder, so do your shopping carefully and decide which materials fit your cooking style as well as your budget.

You must also decide whether to purchase cookware with a nonstick finish. Today's finishes are excellent, saving much clean-up time. I would recommend buying an omelet pan and perhaps a saucepan with a "special" finish. I do prefer having a skillet without a nonstick surface. This utensil tends to give thicker and richer gravy and better browning capabilities. The choice is yours, however. Take a look at your cooking habits and choose accordingly.

COOKWARE ACCESSORIES TO PURCHASE

Rack: A round rack, designed for the placement of food above the bottom of the pan, allows for a great deal of cooking versatility. This accessory is well worth the investment because it converts a pan into a steamer, an oven, or a roaster. Be sure that the rack fits your Dutch oven, wok, and skillet for maximum usage. Also be sure that it will sit at least 1 inch above the bottom of the pan.

Steaming Basket: Generally, the type that folds and fits all your kettles is the most versatile. This accessory can be used for steaming vegetables, meats, and fruits. Again, be sure that the bottom of the basket will sit at least 1 inch above the bottom of the pan.

KITCHEN UTENSILS AND EQUIPMENT USED IN THE RECIPES IN THIS BOOK

Assorted mixing bowls	Measuring cups
Assortment of knives	Measuring spoons
Colander	Meat tenderizing mallet
Cooking spoons	Pancake turner
Custard cups	Rubber spatulas
Cutting board	Sieve

Deep-fat thermometer   Slotted spoon
Electric blender   Steamed pudding mold
Electric toaster   Vegetable parer
Fondue forks   Wire whisk
Grater/shredder

MEASURING MADE EASY

Basic measuring equipment is essential to the success of any recipe. Check to see that you have the proper measuring cups and spoons. You should have:

1 set of measuring spoons, including ¼, ½, 1 teaspoon and 1 tablespoon

Liquid (glass) measuring cups, including 1- , 2- , and 4-cup measures

Dry measuring cups, including ¼- , ⅓- , ½- , and 1-cup measures

It is necessary to have both the liquid and dry measures to be able to measure accurately. The dry measures allow you to level off ingredients with a spatula. The glass measures allow you to see through the cups in order to pour to exactly the correct level.

BASIC MEASURING CHART

Dash/Pinch	less than ⅛ teaspoon
3 teaspoons	1 tablespoon
⅛ cup (1 fluid ounce)	2 tablespoons
¼ cup (2 fluid ounces)	4 tablespoons
⅓ cup	5 tablespoons plus 1 teaspoon
½ cup (4 fluid ounces)	8 tablespoons
⅔ cup	10 tablespoons plus 2 teaspoons
¾ cup (6 fluid ounces)	12 tablespoons
1 cup (8 fluid ounces)	16 tablespoons
2 cups (16 fluid ounces)	1 pint
4 cups (32 fluid ounces)	1 quart
2 pints	1 quart
4 quarts (liquid)	1 gallon
8 quarts (dry)	1 peck
4 pecks	1 bushel
16 ounces (dry measures)	1 pound
1 ounce	28.35 grams
1 pound	453.6 grams

A KITCHEN HELPER TO HAVE ON HAND

Aluminum foil is a boon for many needs that arise during meal preparation. You will find that many of the recipes in this book call for the use of foil. It can act as an additional cooking utensil, keep food warm, and make cleanup easy. It also serves as a container for foods for your freezer, especially helpful if you're cooking for one person.

Now you're ready to go on to the next step. You need only a few handy tips to help you on your way, and some food to put in those pots and pans you just purchased!

Planning: The Key to Culinary Success!

I know you've heard this before, but I'll repeat it because it's true and really imperative. Advanced planning—a week ahead—will help you approach any cooking experience with confidence, be it a *one-burner* recipe or a gourmet meal using every utensil in the house.

Try to sit down a week ahead with your personal calendar and map out the time strategies. See which nights you will be home for dinner and which nights are up for grabs. Take a look at the *Suggested Menus* that appear at the end of most chapters. These menus will give you ideas as you plan the weekly schedule. They are only "suggestions," but they will help the thought process to begin flowing.

Start by selecting the recipes that will fit the bill for the evenings when you're sure you'll be home. Now look at those nights where anything could happen and select recipes from the book containing foods that can be stored on the pantry shelves, ready for a last-minute decision. The *Tin-Can Canteen* and *Hearty Hot Sandwich* chapters (pages 50 and 33) were developed for just such occasions.

Now you can begin to complete the grocery list. Arrange your list according to the way your favorite grocery store is laid out. If you truly want to be organized, make a permanent list that has all the major departments outlined. Duplicate this blank list or keep it on your personal computer. This kind of organization pays benefits later by saving time and saving money because you will be shopping from strength: You know what you need and you have no decisions to suffer through when you start pushing the cart through the grocery store aisles.

Planning may seem a bit time consuming, but I assure you, you'll save a heap of time with blank grocery lists. In fact, if you have a busy family, you'll find that family members will tell you when the last morsel of an item has been used, so that you won't be surprised later when you want to use the item that your child ate last night.

Here are a few additional planning suggestions:

1. Plan your weekly marketing to coincide with the special weekly food section in your local newspaper. Now your choices, especially the costly meat items, can be guided by the specials—the sales items—that are featured. Saving money as well as time is a nice side benefit!

2. Plan to do your marketing at any time the stores are not crowded. Save time by avoiding the "after-work" syndrome. The checkout lines are long, tempers are short—and you'll be hungry. That means you'll buy quick-energy foods that your budget and your figure can't really afford.

USE OF CONVENIENCE FOODS

Why not use the "now" technology by taking advantage of the many packaged foods available on store shelves? I'm not advocating replacing most of your kitchen utensils with a can opener, but there are clever ways to incorporate convenience foods into your cooking style, especially when time is a factor.

Convenience foods, such as salad dressings, canned soups, sauces, gravies, and seasoning mixes, can make your life easier. Combine several packages, cans, or jars to invent your very own convenience foods. To these "helpers" you can add your own creative fresh ingredients to make the dish truly yours. Save additional time by using items such as preminced fresh garlic and frozen chopped onion, chives, and green pepper. They taste as good as fresh, and you'll appreciate the convenience.

Don't ignore the delicatessans as a great source of convenience foods. They can supply you with quick salads, cooked meats for sandwiches and casseroles, fancy breads, and more. Use these delis to buy chicken for chicken à la king or sliced corned beef for a Reuben sandwich.

SIMPLICITY: Handling Accompaniments with the *one-burner*.

One of the best pieces of advice I can share with you is to keep food preparation delicious, creative, and simple. Most of the recipes in this book need only a salad as an accompaniment. This can be a vegetable or fruit salad, depending on the menu.

Many recipes call for rice, pasta, or potatoes to serve with the entrée. If you have the extra burner to cook these in an additional pan, go ahead. If you truly are cooking on a single burner, you might want to make some adjustments, take some shortcuts.

Chow mein noodles are an easy substitute for rice and pasta in some recipes and require only a can opener! Biscuits and patty shells can be purchased at the corner bakery as well as potato baskets (compressed shoestring potatoes). Pasta and rice can be cooked ahead of the entrée and kept warm by covering with foil until the rest of the meal is completed. Cooked pasta can also be easily reheated by running hot tap water over it in a colander.

The *Side-Dish Showstoppers* chapter (page 162) can also offer additional recipes and hints for the preparation of salads, side dishes, sauces, and beverages to serve with your entrée.

ADVANCE PREPARATION

If your schedule is very tight, you may want to select recipes that can be prepared ahead and reheated at a moment's notice. This feature is especially helpful if family members straggle in at odd hours.

Some recipes can be prepared and frozen to accommodate unpredictable schedules. Freeze entrées in serving-size portions for maximum flexibility. Smaller portions defrost quickly for last-minute decisions. Freeze leftovers, too, in serving-size portions for a quick meal for one or two when needed. If you need to feed more than one or two, the defrost time is shorter for smaller packages than it is for larger ones—smaller packages are also easier to store.

If this concept works well for your life-style, consider the purchase of an electric bag sealer. Meals can be packaged, frozen, and reheated in the same bag. The best news is the cleanup. Just toss the bag in the garbage!

PREMEASURING BEFORE BEGINNING TO COOK

For those busy evenings when you come home from work and need the meal prepared quickly, be sure to premeasure your ingredients the day before or that morning. This kind of preparation is especially important with the stir-fry and pasta dishes. You'll be surprised how fast you can pull a meal together if all the ingredients are ready to be cooked. In fact, with some of these recipes, it is imperative that you premeasure all the ingredients before you turn on your burner. Premeasuring is also a help if you plan to entertain after work when time is at a premium before guests arrive.

The key to enjoyable, efficient cooking and dining—even more than creativity—is planning ahead. Eliminate as many last-minute decisions as you can. That way you can more easily cope with each last-minute crisis that's bound to come up. Now you're ready to go on to the next step. You already know what equipment you need and how to organize your menus. Now it's time to have fun. So, happy planning, happy cooking, happy dining!

2

Fabulous Breakfasts and Brunches

It's becoming easier during the week to grab breakfast on the run at any number of the many fast-food outlets. These restaurants can quickly lose their appeal, and the desire to have a quick, but substantial, breakfast at home becomes more important. Steaming French toast, stacks of light pancakes, and hearty omelets are all *one-burner* meals that will begin your day on a very positive note, right in your own kitchen.

But when the weekend comes, additional breakfast choices open before you, with the All-American Brunch. Now you have the time to linger over savory fruit salads, fancy egg dishes, flaky breakfast breads, and lots of piping hot coffee.

Brunch can be served on Saturday or Sunday, between 10:00 A.M. and 3:00 P.M. It can be informal or very elegant, sit-down or buffet. Brunch is perfect for the *one-burner* concept, for egg and creamed entrées are typically cooked in a skillet or frying pan.

Set a pretty table, complete with fresh flowers and bright accessories to make the occasion extra special. Use garnishes whenever color is needed. You'll be surprised how a little splash of red pimiento or green parsley can add that needed touch.

So the next time you promise to entertain, why not choose a weekend brunch? You'll enjoy it as much as your guests.

Egg Basics

The egg has become the most popular ingredient at the American breakfast table. There are many ways to cook that egg and a few hints to doing it correctly and creatively. Here are a few suggestions:

9

FRIED EGGS: Prepared "sunny-side up" or "over easy," this has been a favorite with the heartiest of appetites. Born during the days of country farm breakfasts, the fried egg was cooked in bacon drippings that added a delightful flavor. Today, the health-conscious cook will prepare the fried egg in a pan coated with a nonstick finish and sprayed with a noncaloric vegetable cooking spray.

POACHED EGGS: Gaining popularity due to the lack of additional fats needed to cook the eggs, this technique is easier than most people think. Select a skillet that is not too large for the number of eggs to be cooked. Add enough water to cover the eggs once they're slipped into the pan. Bring the water to a gentle boil, adding a tablespoon of white vinegar to help keep the egg whites together. Slip the eggs into the water one at a time. Spoon hot water over the top of the eggs if not covered. Cook until the eggs reach the desired doneness. Remove the eggs from the pan with a slotted spoon.

If this still seems a bit too much for you, there are poaching rings that can be purchased in gourmet kitchen equipment stores; they will make a perfectly shaped egg.

Poached eggs can be cooked in sauces as well as in simmering water. Creamed mixtures and seasoned tomato sauces are excellent variations to the standard recipe. There are several examples of this technique in this chapter.

SOFT-COOKED EGGS (*cooked in the shell*): A popular breakfast fare that is easy to prepare if timed accurately. Put the eggs in a saucepan of cold water. Cover and bring to a boil. Lower the heat to a simmer and continue to cook for 3 minutes for a soft yolk and 4 minutes for a firmer yolk. Stop the cooking process by plunging the eggs into cold water. Serve in egg cups.

SCRAMBLED EGGS: This is the time to use your sauté or omelet pan with a nonstick finish for best results. With a fork, beat 4 eggs with 2 tablespoons of water and salt and pepper to taste. Melt 1 tablespoon of butter or margarine in a pan over medium-low heat. Add the eggs. Let them set on the bottom. Using a spatula, bring the set eggs to the top of the mixture. Repeat until the eggs are cooked and slightly moist. Serve at once.

Any of the following ingredients can be added to scrambled eggs if desired:

Grated natural cheese

Diced cooked meats, such as ham, prosciutto, bacon bits, and sausages

Smoked salmon

Chopped fresh herbs

Sautéed vegetables

Sun-dried tomatoes, hot peppers, or sliced green onions (scallions)

OMELETS: The omelet is a classic recipe that is popular the world over. It is welcomed at breakfast and brunch, but can make quick work of meal preparation anytime of the day. This versatile entrée can be prepared with or without a filling to suit the occasion. There are many different kinds of omelets from the classic to the puffy varieties. The Classic Omelet is the most popular and appears in this chapter (page 12) with a wide variety of variations. Consult the specific recipe for how-to directions.

Tips for Better Breakfasts on Busy Mornings

With today's hectic schedules, it is hard to find the time to prepare breakfast. The merits of taking the time to have a nutritious breakfast have long been the topic of conversation with dieticians and weight-loss groups, so why not give breakfast a fair chance and start your day on a positive note? This early repast could set the tone for the entire day and save you from the 10:00 A.M. "hungries."

MORE BREAKFAST TIPS

· Plan your meals for the week. Have the groceries on hand, ready for action.

· Stock a variety of choices for the family so picky eaters have no excuses!

· Set the table the evening before to save time and try to include a bouquet of fresh flowers and bright accessories for fun.

· Invite participation in the preparation by family members. Set a schedule and let each member take charge of at least one breakfast a week.

The Classic Omelet

This meal is great any time of the day. Be sure to try the many variations that can make a plain omelet very special.

> *3 large eggs*
> *1 tablespoon water*
> *¼ teaspoon salt*
> *Freshly ground black pepper to taste*
> *2 tablespoons butter or margarine*

1. In a bowl, beat the eggs, water, and seasonings until just blended.
2. In a small frying pan or omelet pan, melt the butter over medium-high heat.
3. Add the eggs, tilting the pan to coat it evenly. Let the mixture set partially before lifting the edges to allow any uncooked egg to flow underneath. Continue to cook until the eggs are set but not dry.
4. Add a filling, if desired, down the center of the omelet, fold the omelet in half over the filling and slide the omelet onto a plate. Serve immediately.

YIELD: 1 serving.

VARIATIONS

Herb—Add 1 tablespoon chopped fresh herbs to egg mixture before cooking. Basil, green onions (scallions), parsley, chives, or thyme are a few you might choose. (See substitution chart [page 208] for using dried herbs.)

Cheese—Add ⅓ cup shredded Cheddar or Gruyère cheese as filling. Fold and cook until cheese melts.

Vegetable—Before cooking omelet, sauté ¼ cup chopped onion and 1 cup of your favorite vegetable combinations, such as sliced mushrooms, diced zucchini, chopped green pepper, cubed eggplant, or chopped tomatoes, in butter or margarine until tender. Set aside while cooking omelet in same pan. Add vegetables as a filling when eggs are set. Fold omelet over filling.

Fruit—Add fresh raspberries or sliced fresh strawberries to cooked omelet. Fold omelet over filling. Top with sour cream.

Meat—Add cooked crumbled bacon, sausage, or ground beef to mixture as eggs set.

Macadamia-Ham—Combine ¼ cup diced cooked ham, 1 tablespoon chopped macadamia nuts, 2 tablespoons crushed pineapple, and 1 tablespoon brown sugar. Add ham mixture to cooked omelet. Fold omelet over filling.

Crab and Artichoke—Add ½ cup flaked crab meat and 1 cooked, quartered artichoke heart to omelet when set. Fold omelet over filling.

TOPPINGS

Choose any of the following toppings to complete your perfect omelet.

- Sour Cream and Chives
- Shredded Cheeses, such as Cheddar, Swiss, mozzarella, or Muenster
- Herbed Tomato Sauce (15-ounce can), heated
- Packaged Sauces, such as cheese or Hollandaise
- Fruit Preserves

Blintz Omelet

If you've ever had a blintz, you'll appreciate this recipe. The fruit, cheese, and egg combination is delightful for breakfast or brunch. Serve it with fresh fruit and flaky biscuits.

> *6 large eggs*
> *2 tablespoons milk*
> *Salt to taste*
> *Pinch of freshly ground black pepper*
> *½ cup cream-style cottage cheese*
> *2 tablespoons butter or margarine*
> *⅔ cup fruit preserves of your choice*

1. In a mixing bowl, beat the eggs, milk, salt, and pepper together until foamy. Stir in the cottage cheese.

2. Preheat a frying pan over medium heat; then add the butter. When it has melted, pour the egg mixture into the skillet. Lower the heat and cook, without stirring, until the bottom of the mixture is set. Lift the edges and let any uncooked egg flow to the bottom. Cook until the top of the omelet is set.
3. Spread the omelet with the preserves and fold the omelet in half. Remove to a serving platter and serve immediately.

YIELD: 2 servings.

Breakfast Frittata

This frittata has all the fixings for a hearty breakfast feast, but it makes a great dish for any meal of the day.

> *2 tablespoons butter or margarine*
> *½ cup sliced fresh mushrooms*
> *½ cup chopped sweet green pepper*
> *¼ cup chopped onion*
> *6 large eggs*
> *2 tablespoons water*
> *½ cup diced ham*
> *4 ounces Cheddar cheese,*
> * shredded*

1. In a frying pan, melt the butter over medium heat. Sauté the mushrooms, green pepper, and onion until tender.
2. In a mixing bowl, beat the eggs and water until foamy. Stir in the ham.
3. Pour the egg mixture into the skillet over the vegetables. Let the eggs set on the bottom; then lift the edges to allow any uncooked egg to flow underneath. Cover and cook until the eggs are set, about 3 minutes.
4. Sprinkle with the cheese and cut into wedges to serve.

YIELD: 4 servings.

Cajun Eggs

This recipe uses hard-cooked eggs for a nice change of pace. When time is short, and you want a colorful brunch idea, try this. Serve it with hot cooked rice and a dessert of fresh fruit for a delightful and colorful meal.

> *2 tablespoons butter or margarine*
> *1 large onion, chopped*
> *1 medium-size sweet green pepper, chopped*
> *1 garlic clove, minced*
> *1 teaspoon salt*
> *Pinch of dried thyme*
> *Pinch of dried rosemary, crumbled*
> *Pinch of paprika*
> *Pinch of cayenne pepper, or to taste*
> *1 14½-ounce can tomatoes, chopped and liquid reserved*
> *8 hard-cooked eggs, cooled, shelled, and cut in half lengthwise*
> *1 4½-ounce can small shrimp, drained*

1. In a frying pan, melt the butter over medium heat. Sauté the onion, green pepper, and garlic until tender.
2. Add the seasonings and tomatoes and liquid. Cover and simmer for 15 minutes.
3. Stir in the eggs and shrimp. Heat through.

YIELD: 4 to 6 servings.

Mushroom-Sauced Eggs

If you like fresh mushrooms and poached eggs, this is the dish for you.

> *¼ cup butter or margarine*
> *½ pound fresh mushrooms, sliced*
> *½ small onion, chopped*
> *¼ cup all-purpose flour*
> *¼ teaspoon salt*
> *1 cup half-and-half*
> *1 cup canned chicken broth*
> *6 to 8 large eggs*
> *3 to 4 split English muffins, toasted*
> *Freshly ground black pepper*
> *Chopped fresh parsley leaves*

1. In a frying pan, melt the butter over medium heat. Sauté the mushrooms and onions until they are soft.
2. Add the flour and salt and blend well. Stir in the cream and chicken broth and cook and stir until thickened.
3. Carefully drop the eggs from a small cup, one at a time, into the mushroom sauce. Cover and cook over low heat until the eggs reach the desired doneness, about 3 to 5 minutes.
4. Spoon an egg over a muffin half and top with the mushroom sauce. Garnish with ground pepper and chopped parsley.

YIELD: 3 to 4 servings.

Italian Poached Eggs

This is a unique way to serve eggs for brunch.

2 cups One-Hour Spaghetti Sauce (page 108, see Note)
8 large eggs
8 slices Italian bread, toasted, or 4 English muffins, halved and toasted
Grated Parmesan cheese

1. In a frying pan, heat the sauce to a simmer. Carefully slide the eggs into the sauce, one at a time. Cover and simmer until the eggs are cooked to the desired doneness, about 3 minutes.
2. Place a cooked egg on a toasted bread slice or English muffin half and top with the sauce. Sprinkle with grated cheese and serve immediately.

YIELD: 4 servings.

NOTE: Use prepared bottled sauce if desired.

Eggs Olé

For a midday brunch, this dish is simple and colorful. Serve the eggs on warmed soft flour tortillas for real Mexican flavor or toasted English muffin halves.

1 tablespoon butter or margarine
1 sweet green pepper, chopped
1 small onion, chopped
¼ cup diced green chiles, or to taste
4 medium-size ripe tomatoes, diced
Salt and freshly ground black pepper to taste
8 slices Monterey Jack cheese
8 large eggs

1. In a frying pan, melt the butter over medium heat. Sauté
   the green pepper, onion, and chiles until soft. Add the tomatoes and seasonings. Cook until thickened.
2. Lay the cheese slices on top of the tomato mixture.
3. Carefully drop the eggs from a small cup, one at a time, on
   top of each slice of cheese.
4. Cover the pan and simmer until the eggs are cooked to the
   desired doneness, about 3 minutes. Use a pancake turner to
   remove each serving from the pan. Serve immediately.

YIELD: 4 servings.

Eggs Goldenrod

This recipe is a perfect way to use hard-cooked eggs. Although
it's a wonderful brunch meal, I often serve it for supper when
fresh asparagus is in season. Just add cut, cooked asparagus to
the sauce in step 3.

¼ cup butter or margarine
¼ cup all-purpose flour
2 cups milk
1 tablespoon Dijon mustard
Salt and freshly ground black pepper to taste
4 hard-cooked eggs
8 toast points, or 8 toasted English muffin halves
2 tablespoons chopped fresh parsley leaves
Paprika

1. In a saucepan, melt the butter over medium heat. Add the
   flour, stirring constantly to form a smooth paste.
2. Add the milk gradually and cook, stirring constantly, until
   the mixture thickens; then add the mustard and seasonings.

3. Shell the eggs and separate the whites from the yolks. Chop the whites and add them to the saucepan. Heat through.
4. Serve the sauce over toast points. Garnish with chopped parsley, sieved egg yolks, and a sprinkling of paprika.

YIELD: 4 servings.

No-Crust Quiche

There's no need to turn on the oven to prepare this quiche.

> *2 tablespoons butter or margarine*
> *3 green onions (scallions), sliced*
> *6 large eggs*
> *1 8-ounce package cream cheese, softened*
> *1 cup milk*
> *1 3-ounce jar real crumbled bacon*
> *1 cup shredded Cheddar cheese*
> *¹/₂ teaspoon dried basil*
> *¹/₄ teaspoon freshly ground black pepper*

1. In a frying pan, melt the butter over medium heat. Sauté the onions until they are soft.
2. Meanwhile, beat the eggs, cream cheese, and milk until smooth. Stir in the remaining ingredients.
3. Pour the egg mixture into the frying pan. Cook, covered, over medium heat until the eggs are set, about 15 to 20 minutes. Cut into wedges to serve.

YIELD: 6 servings.

Farmer's Breakfast

This dish includes all you will need to serve except, perhaps, a dish of fresh fruit and a sweet roll.

> *3 tablespoons butter or margarine*
> *3 medium-size potatoes, peeled and sliced thin*
> *4 green onions (scallions), sliced*

½ *sweet green pepper, diced*
2 *cups diced ham*
Salt and freshly ground black pepper to taste
4 *large eggs, beaten*
4 *ounces Cheddar cheese, shredded*

1. In a frying pan, melt the butter over medium heat. Sauté the vegetables, ham, and seasonings for 3 minutes. Cover and cook over low heat until the potatoes are tender, about 30 minutes.
2. Pour the eggs over the vegetables. Do not stir. Cover and cook until the eggs are set, about 10 minutes.
3. Sprinkle with the cheese and heat only until the cheese melts. Cut into wedges to serve.

YIELD: 4 servings.

Sausage and Potato Brunch Pie

This hearty dish can be served at any time of the day. The breakfast sausages add a delightful seasoning to this recipe.

6 *large eggs, beaten*
1 *teaspoon onion powder*
Pinch of freshly ground black pepper
3 *cups frozen hash brown potatoes with peppers and onions (see Note)*
4 *ounces Cheddar cheese, shredded*
8 *ounces breakfast sausages, cooked and sliced* ¼ *inch thick, or 8 ounces Old-Fashioned Breakfast Sausage Patties (page 27), cooked and crumbled*
1 *ripe tomato, sliced*

1. In a mixing bowl, combine all the ingredients except the tomato.
2. Preheat a well-greased 9- or 10-inch frying pan over medium heat. Add the mixture, cover, and cook for 20 to 25 minutes, or until brown on the bottom and set on the top.

3. Place a dinner plate or platter over the frying pan. Using hot pads, flip the omelet over onto the platter. Cut into wedges and garnish with fresh tomato slices.

YIELD: 6 servings.

NOTE: If desired, raw potatoes can be used in place of the frozen hash browns. Add onion and chopped sweet red and green pepper to taste. Sauté until the vegetables are soft; then proceed as directed above.

Ceal's Cheese Blintzes

If you're looking for an elegant brunch that can be prepared ahead, this is the recipe for you.

BLINTZ CRÊPES

³/₄ cup cornstarch
¹/₂ teaspoon salt
1³/₄ cups cold water
6 large eggs, beaten
Vegetable oil

1. In a mixing bowl, dissolve the cornstarch and salt in the cold water. Add the eggs and stir well.
2. Preheat a 6-inch sauté or omelet pan over medium-high heat. Grease the pan using paper towels to spread the oil. Wipe off any excess.
3. When the pan is heated and oiled, pour 2 tablespoons of batter into the pan and quickly tilt the pan to coat the entire bottom. Pour any excess batter back into the mixing bowl.
4. Return the pan to the heat and cook until the crêpes are lightly browned on the bottom. Remove to brown paper to drain. Repeat the procedure, greasing and wiping out the pan for each crêpe. Stir the batter occasionally. The crêpes may be stacked when cool. If the batter becomes thick before all the crêpes are made, stir in ¹/₄ cup of water.

CHEESE FILLING

23 ounces skim-milk ricotta cheese (1 15-ounce and 1 8-ounce
    carton)
1 8-ounce package cream cheese, softened
4 large eggs
¼ to ½ cup sugar
2 teaspoons salt

Butter or margarine
Sour cream
Canned cherry or blueberry pie filling

1. In a mixing bowl, cream the cheeses together until smooth.
2. Add the eggs one at a time; then add the remaining ingredients.
3. Place 1 heaping teaspoon of the filling on each crêpe, cooked side up, and fold envelope style. Each blintz should be 2 inches by 1 inch.
4. When ready to serve, melt 1 to 2 tablespoons of butter in a frying pan over medium-high heat. Sauté the blintzes until lightly browned on both sides.
5. Serve immediately with sour cream and cherry or blueberry pie filling.

YIELD: 48 blintzes.

NOTE: This recipe can be prepared ahead and refrigerated or frozen to the point of sautéing. When stacking filled blintz crêpes for freezing, use wax paper between layers.

Basic Crêpes

The batter should be the consistency of whipping cream. For real convenience, prepare it ahead and store, covered, in the refrigerator. The batter will keep for several days.

3 large eggs
1½ cups milk
3 tablespoons butter or margarine, melted
1 cup all-purpose flour
½ teaspoon salt
Vegetable oil

1. Combine all the ingredients in a blender or a mixing bowl with a wire whisk. Let the batter stand for 1 hour before using.
2. Preheat a 6-inch sauté pan over medium-high heat. When the pan is hot enough to sizzle a drop of water, use a paper towel to rub a generous amount of oil over the inside of the pan.
3. Quickly pour a scant ¼ cup of batter into the pan. Tip and swirl the pan to coat the inside. If any batter remains, pour back into the remaining batter.
4. Return the pan to the heat and cook until the crêpe is lightly browned on the bottom.
5. Slip onto wax paper and allow to cool before stacking with paper dividers. Fill or refrigerate until ready to use.

YIELD: 24 crêpes.

Filling Suggestions

Brunch and Main Dish Ideas

Sausages and Apples (page 28)

Chicken and Mushrooms à la King (page 27)

Mexican Scramble (page 80)

Beef Burgundy Slimmer (page 81)

Cajun Eggs (page 14)

Dessert Ideas

Fill crêpes with ice cream and top with Chocolate-Caramel Rum Sauce (page 203)

Fill crêpes with vanilla ice cream and top with Bananas Flambé (page 183)

Fill crêpes with vanilla ice cream and top with Peach Melba Sundae sauce (page 195)

Fill crêpes with sautéed apples and top with Rum Custard Sauce (page 182)

Raisin-Nut French Toast

Try this variation of an old favorite or use white bread if you like the traditional French toast. The unusual twist is to top your toast with plain yogurt and sliced fresh strawberries. If you're a purist, butter and syrup are very good, too.

> 1 large egg
> ½ cup milk
> 1 teaspoon sugar
> 1 teaspoon vanilla extract
> 2 tablespoons butter or margarine
> 4 slices raisin-nut bread

1. In a shallow bowl, beat the egg, milk, sugar, and vanilla together.
2. In a frying pan or griddle, melt the butter over medium heat.
3. Dip the bread, one slice at a time, in the egg mixture and then place it in the hot pan. Cook until brown on both sides.

YIELD: 2 servings.

ENTERTAINING HINT: For a pretty presentation buy a round loaf of cinnamon-raisin-nut bread. Arrange prepared bread rounds overlapping in a circle design on each serving plate. Top with a dollop of whipped butter in the center of each serving.

Stuffed French Toast

What could be better than French toast with a surprise inside? Serve these with butter and syrup.

> 3 tablespoons butter or margarine
> 1 baking apple, peeled, cored, and sliced thin
> 1 tablespoon brown sugar
> 4 slices whole wheat, white, or French bread
> 1 large egg, beaten
> ¼ cup milk
> 1 teaspoon vanilla extract

1. In a frying pan, melt 1 tablespoon of the butter over medium heat. Sauté the apple and brown sugar until the apple is soft.
2. Divide the apple mixture between 2 slices of the bread. Top with the remaining bread. Wipe the pan clean.
3. Combine the egg, milk, and vanilla. Dip each side of the sandwiches in the egg mixture.
4. Heat the frying pan or griddle over medium-high heat. Melt the remaining 2 tablespoons of butter.
5. Brown the sandwiches on both sides and serve immediately.

YIELD: 2 servings.

Sticky Cinnamon Toast

What nicer way to face a cold winter day than with the taste and aroma of hot cinnamon! Served with applesauce, prunes, or figs, it will start the day with a cozy warm feeling.

> *¹/₄ cup butter or margarine, softened*
> *¹/₄ cup packed brown sugar*
> *1 teaspoon ground cinnamon*
> *4 slices French bread, 1 inch thick*

1. In a small bowl, combine the butter, sugar, and cinnamon. Spread the butter mixture on both sides of each slice of bread.
2. Preheat a frying pan or griddle over medium heat. Grill the bread slices until brown on both sides.

YIELD: 2 servings.

Cornmeal Country Pancakes

This is my favorite recipe for pancakes. Buttermilk adds a delightful tang, and cornmeal, a great texture. Serve them with the traditional syrup and butter, or top them with a purchased berry fruit sauce.

1¾ cups yellow cornmeal
1 teaspoon salt
¾ teaspoon baking soda
⅓ cup all-purpose flour
2 large eggs
2¼ cups buttermilk
⅓ cup vegetable oil

1. Combine the dry ingredients in a mixing bowl.
2. Beat the eggs, buttermilk, and oil together until well mixed.
   Combine the liquid and dry ingredients.
3. Heat a greased griddle or large frying pan over medium-high
   heat. Using ¼ cup batter per pancake, cook until each is
   golden brown and bubbles form on the surface. Turn and
   brown the other side.

YIELD: 20 to 24 4-inch pancakes.

Flapjacks

These pancakes are light and a perfect candidate for the addition
to the batter of fresh blueberries or chopped pecans. Serve them
with syrup and butter.

1½ cups all-purpose flour
1 teaspoon salt
2 tablespoons sugar
2 teaspoons baking powder
1¼ cups milk
2 large eggs, lightly beaten
3 tablespoons butter, melted

1. Combine the dry ingredients in a mixing bowl.
2. Combine the milk, eggs, and butter. Then combine the liquid
   and dry ingredients.
3. Heat a greased griddle or large frying pan over medium-high
   heat. Using ¼ cup per pancake, cook until bubbles form on
   the surface of each pancake. Turn and cook other side.

YIELD: 16 4-inch pancakes.

Buttermilk English Muffins

There is nothing like the taste of homemade English muffins. Baked on a griddle, they are the easiest of the yeast breads to prepare. This recipe has an unusual twist because it is a batter bread.

1 1/4-ounce package fast-rising yeast
1/2 teaspoon sugar
3/4 cup warm water (110 to 115 degrees)
1 cup buttermilk
2 cups all-purpose flour
1/2 teaspoon salt
1/2 teaspoon baking soda
Vegetable cooking spray

1. In a small bowl, combine the yeast and sugar with 1/4 cup of the warm water. Set aside until the mixture foams, about 10 minutes.
2. Heat the buttermilk until it is just warm.
3. Put the flour and salt into a large mixing bowl. Add the yeast mixture and warm buttermilk. Beat by hand until smooth and elastic, about 3 minutes.
4. Cover and let rise in a warm place until doubled, about 30 minutes.
5. Combine the baking soda and remaining 1/2 cup of water. Add to the dough and beat until well mixed. Cover and let rise in a warm place for 15 minutes.
6. Heat a griddle over medium-high heat. Turn the heat to low and grease the griddle with vegetable cooking spray. Spray the inside of 3- to 4-inch muffin rings or tuna cans with the vegetable cooking spray (see Note). Place on the griddle.
7. Fill each ring with enough batter to make a 1/2-inch depth. Spread the batter evenly within the ring.
8. Cook until the batter doubles in height and is lightly brown on the underside, about 8 minutes. Remove each ring with tongs. Turn each muffin with a metal spatula. Cook until brown. Remove to a wire rack. Repeat the process until all the batter is used. Regrease the rings each time they are used.
9. To serve, split the muffins with a fork. Toast and top with butter and jam.

YIELD: 12 to 16 muffins.

NOTE: Save tuna, water chestnut, or similar-size cans to make your own rings. Open both ends and wash well.

Chicken and Mushrooms à la King

This is a perfect entrée for that "special" brunch or even a luncheon. This recipe can be prepared ahead and reheated just before serving for a real time-saver. If desired, you can substitute 3 cups of cooked seafood of your choice for the chicken.

> *¼ cup butter or margarine*
> *½ pound fresh mushrooms, sliced*
> *3 tablespoons all-purpose flour*
> *1 cup canned chicken broth*
> *1 cup milk*
> *¼ teaspoon dried thyme*
> *Pinch of freshly ground black pepper*
> *3 cups cubed cooked chicken*
> *¼ cup dry sherry*
> *6 prepared patty shells*

1. In a frying pan, melt the butter over medium heat. Sauté the mushrooms for 3 minutes. Add the flour and blend well.
2. Stir in the chicken broth and milk and cook and stir until thickened.
3. Add the seasonings, chicken cubes, and sherry. Heat through and serve hot over the patty shells.

YIELD: 6 to 8 servings.

NOTE: This recipe can be used to fill the Basic Crêpes (page 21), making 8 servings or 16 crêpes.

Old-Fashioned Breakfast Sausage Patties

You can enjoy homemade sausage without having to prepare great quantities. Simply mix already ground pork with herbs and spices and shape into serving-size portions. Enjoy some now and freeze the rest for future feasting.

> *2 pounds unseasoned ground pork*
> *2 garlic cloves, minced*
> *2 teaspoons ground sage*
> *1 teaspoon freshly ground black pepper*
> *¹/₄ teaspoon dried thyme*
> *¹/₄ teaspoon hot red pepper flakes, or to taste*
> *Salt to taste*

1. Combine all the ingredients in a bowl. Cover and refrigerate at least several hours or overnight to allow the flavors to mingle.
2. Use ¹/₃ cup of the mixture to make each patty.
3. In a skillet or frying pan, fry the patties until brown on both sides and well done.

YIELD: 10 patties.

Sausages and Apples

This is a wonderful morning treat, ready quickly if brown and serve sausages are used. Serve with pancakes, scrambled eggs, or simply with toasted English muffins. I have also used this as a filling for Basic Crêpes (page 21).

8 ounces pork breakfast sausages (8 links), or 4 Old-Fashioned Breakfast Sausage Patties (preceding recipe)
1 small onion, sliced
2 apples, peeled, cored, and sliced
Pinch of ground cinnamon

1. In a frying pan, brown the sausages and onion over medium heat.
2. Add the apples and sauté until the apples are soft. Sprinkle with cinnamon and serve.

YIELD: 4 servings.

Potato Nests

This is the kind of breakfast that will please even those who shy away from eating in the morning. This recipe is written for any number of servings. Simply prepare as many patties as there are people (unless, of course, they are very hearty eaters). Kids will especially love this recipe!

> *Butter or margarine*
> *Hash brown potato patties*
> *1 egg for each serving*
> *Salt and freshly ground black*
> * pepper*

1. In a frying pan, melt the butter over medium heat. Brown the patties on both sides.
2. With a spoon, make an indentation in the center of each patty. Slip an egg into the depression. Season with salt and pepper, cover and cook until the desired doneness is reached. Serve immediately.

Hot Spiced Shredded Wheat

On a cold winter morning this hot cereal is quick to serve and keeps the children (and you!) warm in the face of the cold winds.

> *1 large shredded wheat biscuit*
> *1 cup milk, warmed*
> *Ground cinnamon and sugar to taste*
> *1 tablespoon butter or margarine*

Put the cereal in a serving bowl and pour the hot milk over it. Sprinkle with the cinnamon and sugar and top with a pat of butter.

YIELD: 1 serving.

SUGGESTED
BREAKFAST AND BRUNCH MENUS

· *A ZIPPY EYE OPENER* ·
Fresh Orange Juice
Raisin-Nut French Toast (page 23)
Beverage

· *OLD-FASHIONED BUT DELICIOUS* ·
Fresh Strawberries and Cream
Cornmeal Country Pancakes (page 24)
Syrup or Fruit Sauce
Old-Fashioned Breakfast Sausage Patties (page 27)
Beverage

· *BRUNCH ON THE LIGHT SIDE* ·
Sliced Fresh Fruit Platter
Eggs Goldenrod (page 17)
Buttermilk English Muffins (page 26)
Beverage

· *A HEARTY BREAKFAST THAT THE KIDS WILL LOVE* ·
Cantaloupe or Grapefruit
Potato Nests (page 29)
Whole Wheat Toast
Jams or Jellies
Beverage

SUGGESTED
BRUNCH MENUS

· *FOR A FESTIVE FLAVOR* ·
Champagne
Fresh Fruit Compote (page 187)
Chicken and Mushrooms à la King (page 27)
Patty Shells
Caramel-Peach Upside-Down Cake (page 196)
Beverage

· *FOR THE HEARTY APPETITE* ·
Bloody Mary
Sausage and Potato Brunch Pie (page 19)
Baking Powder Biscuits
Butter
Jam
Autumn Baked Apples (page 183)
Beverage

· *BRUNCH WITH A CONTINENTAL AIR* ·
Strawberries with Raspberry Purée (page 185)
Mushroom-Sauced Eggs (page 15)
Buttermilk English Muffins (page 26)
Beverage

· *SOUTH OF THE BORDER BRUNCH* ·

Sangria

Eggs Olé (page 16)

Flour Tortillas

Fruit Fritters (page 186)

Coffee Cake

Beverage

3

The Hearty Hot Sandwich

History credits the Earl of Sandwich for starting a revolution in eating by placing a piece of meat between two pieces of bread so that he could eat while continuing to play cards. From that date forward, the sandwich became a toteable fast food served anytime of the day, at casual or formal occasions alike. Today, Americans use the sandwich to fill the lunch box, to entertain guests, to pack in picnic baskets, to warm the family after winter sports, or just to feed a hungry crowd on a busy day.

In most cases, sandwich preparation requires only a few simple ingredients, most already stored on the pantry shelf waiting for the need to arise. Many recipes in this chapter can be prepared in less than 15 minutes and, of course, you need only *One Burner* and a griddle or skillet to perform the magic!

Accompaniments to the Sandwich

A bowl or cup of soup is a perfect companion to the hearty sandwich. Select a soup that complements the flavors in the sandwich. Add a few crispy garnishes, such as carrot and celery sticks, and the meal is complete.

Secrets to Super Hot Grilled Sandwiches

Terrific grilled sandwiches start with a little imagination, a few fresh ingredients, and some basic utensils.

UTENSILS: A heavy skillet or large griddle is all one needs to prepare grilled sandwiches. The heavier the gauge of the pan the better the heat conduction; in the case of the griddle, the thicker the gauge the less chance of warping while cooking over high heat.

Special sandwich grills are also good for the top of the range or as small portable appliances. These delightful grills toast the bread, warm the filling, seal the bread to form an individual pie, and add a decorative design to the exterior of the sandwich.

For hefty sandwiches, it is common practice to weight down the top of the bread during cooking with a bacon press, a heatproof heavy plate, or even a small skillet, leaving enough room around the sandwich for the steam to escape.

If using an electric skillet or griddle, follow manufacturer's directions.

BREAD: Any type of bread can be used. Select the kind of bread to complement the filling. Whole wheat, cracked wheat, and mixed grain breads develop a delightfully nutty flavor when grilled. Look for sources of ethnic breads that are available in your area or bake your own if you're so inclined. The better the quality bread, the better the final product. Here are a few ideas to start your creative juices flowing:

> Cheddar cheese bread
>
> Cracked wheat bread
>
> Dijon-rye bread
>
> French or Italian bread
>
> Herb bread
>
> Pumpernickel-rye bread
>
> Sourdough bread

CHEESE: Most cheeses can be used for grilling inside a sandwich. Cheese helps to bind the sandwich. Look for the more unusual varieties, such as Monterey Jack, Muenster, and mozzarella, to add interest to the meal. Even the more gourmet cheeses, such as Brie, fontina, and pepper, can be used. Be adventurous! Note: Parmesan, feta, and blue cheeses are not recommended for grilled sandwiches.

MEAT FILLINGS: The sky is the limit with meat fillings. Sliced cold meats are a favorite and can be a great way to use leftovers from a roast or cooked chicken or turkey. Your local delicatessen is a good source of sliced meats, too. The nice feature of using the deli is the fact that you can purchase just what you need. Look for a variety of cheeses there, too.

Spreads, such as chicken, egg, and tuna salads, make tasty fillings for grilled sandwiches. Spreads should be thick and creamy to ensure the sandwich will hold together. The addition of a slice of cheese will add extra insurance, as well as flavor.

One final word on grilled sandwiches: Serve them immediately because they do not hold well.

Creative Sandwich Ideas

Besides the many ideas in this chapter, there are other recipes in this book that will easily convert to delicious sandwiches:

MEAT LOAF SANDWICH: Prepare Meat Loaves with Pesto Sauce as directed on page 106. Chill and slice ½ inch thick. Serve on crisp crusty Italian bread.

MUSTARD-HERB CHICKEN BREAST SANDWICH: Prepare Mustard-Herb Chicken Breasts as directed on page 129. Serve with lettuce, tomato, and mayonnaise on a hard roll.

RATATOUILLE AND SAUSAGE SANDWICH: Prepare Ratatouille and Sausage Casserole as directed on page 115. Serve vegetables and sausage warm on French bread. Top with grated Parmesan cheese.

CHILI PITAS: Prepare Lots o' Chili as directed on page 108. Fill a halved pita bread with warmed chili. Top with shredded Cheddar cheese.

PEPPER STEAK PITAS: Prepare Pepper and Tomato Steak as directed on page 148. Fill halved pita breads.

CONEY ISLAND SANDWICH: Prepare Lots o' Chili as directed on page 108. Warm good-quality frankfurters and put them on French rolls. Top with a generous scoop of chili.

Reuben Sandwich

This traditional sandwich is, indeed, a filling meal. Cook your own corned beef over low heat for hours or buy it cooked and sliced from the delicatessen.

> *4 slices dark rye bread*
> *¼ cup bottled Thousand Island salad dressing*
> *4 slices Swiss cheese*
> *¼ to ½ pound corned beef, sliced*
> *1 8-ounce can sauerkraut, well drained*
> *Butter or margarine*

1. Spread one side of each slice of bread with the dressing.
2. Put a slice of cheese and equal amounts of the beef and sauerkraut on 2 bread slices. Top with the remaining cheese and bread.
3. Heat a griddle or frying pan over medium heat. Butter the outsides of the bread slices and grill the sandwiches until they are golden brown on both sides.

YIELD: 2 servings.

Steak and Gravy Sandwich

A substantial meal that's complete when served with a green salad.

> *2 slices white or French bread*
> *3 tablespoons butter or margarine*
> *2 beef cube steaks (about 6 ounces each)*
> *1 teaspoon instant beef bouillon granules*
> *⅓ cup water*
> *2 teaspoons all-purpose flour*
> *1 4-ounce can sliced mushrooms,*
> *   drained*

1. Toast the bread and butter it, if desired. Place on serving dishes.
2. In a skillet, melt the butter over medium heat. Sauté the steaks for 1 minute on each side, or until the desired doneness is reached. Place on the toasted bread.

3. Turn the heat to medium-low. In a measuring cup, combine the bouillon granules, water, and flour. Pour the mixture into the skillet. Stir and cook until thickened.
4. Add the mushrooms and heat through. Pour the gravy over the steaks and serve immediately.

YIELD: 2 servings.

Indonesian Beef in Pita Bread

Here's a spicy change of pace from hamburgers.

> *1 pound lean ground beef*
> *1 small onion, chopped*
> *1 medium-size apple, chopped*
> *¼ cup dark raisins*
> *1 teaspoon salt*
> *l teaspoon curry powder*
> *6 pita (pocket) breads*
> *1 8-ounce container plain yogurt*

1. In a frying pan, cook the beef and onion over medium heat until browned. Drain off any excess fat.
2. Add the apple, raisins, and seasonings. Turn the heat to low, cover, and simmer until the apple is crisp-tender.
3. Cut each pita in half to make 2 pockets. Fill each half with the hot meat mixture. Spoon 1 to 2 tablespoons of yogurt over the filling and serve immediately.

YIELD: 6 servings.

Mexi-Joes

Here's a taco salad on a bun.

> *1 pound lean ground beef*
> *1 package taco seasoning mix*
> *1 cup crushed corn chips*
> *6 hard rolls or buns, split and toasted, if desired*
> *1 cup shredded Cheddar cheese*
> *1 cup chopped ripe tomato*
> *2 cups shredded lettuce*
> *Bottled taco sauce*

1. In a frying pan, brown the beef over medium heat. Drain off any excess fat. Add the taco seasoning mix following package directions.
2. Just before serving, stir in the corn chips. Spoon the mixture onto the split rolls and top with the cheese, tomato, shredded lettuce, and taco sauce.

YIELD: 6 servings.

Zesty Sloppy Joes

Barbecue sauce makes the difference in this version of the American teen favorite. Vary the zest with the brand of barbecue sauce you choose.

> *1 pound lean ground beef*
> *1 cup bottled barbecue sauce*
> *¹/₄ cup chopped sweet green pepper*
> *¹/₄ cup chopped onion*
> *6 hard rolls or buns, split and toasted, if desired*

1. In a frying pan, brown the beef over medium heat. Drain off any excess fat.
2. Add the barbecue sauce, green pepper, and onion. Cover and simmer over low heat for 10 minutes. Serve on the split rolls.

YIELD: 6 servings.

Gourmet Hamburgers

Everyone knows how to prepare the basic, everyday burger, but here are a few ideas that suggest an interesting change of pace. Note the addition of water to the basic recipe; it keeps the burger moist.

BASIC ¹/₄-POUND BURGER

> *1 pound lean ground beef (ground round or ground sirloin)*
> *¹/₄ cup water*
> *Salt and freshly ground black pepper to taste*
> *2 tablespoons butter or margarine*
> *4 hard rolls, split and toasted*

1. Mix the first 3 ingredients together and gently shape them into 4 patties about ½ inch thick. Do not overhandle or the burger will become very firm.
2. In a frying pan, melt the butter over medium-high heat. Sauté the burgers for 5 minutes. Turn and continue to fry for 4 to 5 minutes longer for medium-well done.
3. Serve with your favorite condiments on a hard roll, or a slice of French bread and a pat of butter.

YIELD: 4 servings.

VARIATIONS

Greek Connection—Marinate the uncooked burgers in Italian salad dressing before cooking. Cook as directed above. Top the cooked burgers with red onion slices, sliced ripe (black) olives, and crumbled feta cheese.

Peppercorn Burgers—After shaping the burgers, roll them in freshly cracked black peppercorns. Fry the burgers as directed above.

Mushroom-Swiss Delight—Sauté fresh mushrooms in garlic and butter. Pile on the burger and top with slices of Swiss cheese just before the burgers are done.

Burgers Florentine—Top cooked burgers with chopped fresh tomato, fresh spinach leaves, and a thick, creamy garlic or Parmesan cheese salad dressing.

Burgers Italiano—Season the beef with 1 teaspoon dried oregano, ½ teaspoon dried basil, and a pinch of garlic salt. Mix well before shaping. Fry as directed above. Top the almost-cooked burger with a slice of mozzarella cheese and a slice of ripe tomato.

B-L-T Burgers—Top each cooked burger with several strips of crisp bacon, a lettuce leaf, and a slice of ripe tomato.

Burgers Olé—Top the burgers in their final stage of cooking with a slice of Monterey Jack cheese. Then add a generous dollop of spicy guacamole, diced ripe tomato, and shredded lettuce.

Shredded Beef Sandwich

This recipe is the ultimate in convenience for serving a few or a crowd. Prepare it ahead and simply reheat only the portions needed. The rich, beefy flavor of the meat and gravy makes a hearty meal that requires only a crisp roll to serve it on and a few crunchy vegetables for garnish.

> *2 tablespoons butter or margarine*
> *2 tablespoons olive oil*
> *3 to 4 pounds boneless beef rump roast*
> *1 garlic clove*
> *Salt and freshly ground black pepper*
> *⅓ cup Cognac*
> *2 cups canned beef broth*
> *2 to 3 cups dry red table wine*
> *Crusty French rolls*
> *Sour cream*

1. In a Dutch oven, heat the butter and oil over medium-high heat. Rub the roast with the garlic and season with salt and pepper. Brown the meat on all sides.
2. Add the Cognac to the pan and carefully ignite it with a long match. When the flames die down, add the beef broth and a cup of wine. Cover and simmer until the meat is tender, about 2½ to 3 hours. Add more wine if the liquid begins to evaporate.
3. When tender, remove the roast to a platter and cool to room temperature. Cut the roast into 2-inch slices across the grain. Then pull the slices apart with the grain, producing shreds.
4. Return the meat to the pan juices. Refrigerate, covered, until ready to reheat and serve.
5. To serve, reheat all or a portion of the mixture. Serve on crusty French rolls and top with a dollop of sour cream.

YIELD: 8 to 10 servings.

NOTE: This recipe freezes well for several weeks.

Gyros

This well-seasoned sandwich is a combination of lamb, herbs, cucumbers, and yogurt.

1 tablespoon vegetable oil
¾ pound boneless lamb (shoulder cut), cut into very thin strips of
1½ inches by ½ inch
1 medium-size onion, sliced
1 medium-size cucumber, peeled, seeded, and sliced into crescents
2 pita (pocket) breads
Yogurt-Herb Dressing (page 170)

1. In a frying pan or wok, heat the oil over high heat. Sauté the lamb and onion until the meat is no longer pink. Add the cucumber and cook for 1 minute.
2. Cut the pita breads in half and stuff each half with one fourth of the meat mixture. Pass the Yogurt-Herb Dressing at the table.

YIELD: 4 servings.

Cheesy French Toast

French toast goes to lunch!

8 ounces mozzarella cheese, sliced
4 slices Italian bread, ½ inch thick
1 large egg, beaten
2 tablespoons milk
1 garlic clove, sliced in half
1 tablespoon vegetable oil

1. Divide half the cheese between 2 slices of bread. Top with the remaining bread.
2. Combine the egg and milk in a shallow bowl.
3. Heat a frying pan over medium-high heat. Sauté the garlic in the oil until it is brown; then discard the garlic.
4. Dip both sandwiches in the egg mixture and grill until golden brown on both sides, turning once.

YIELD: 2 servings.

Beer and Brats

Because my father is a brewer, this recipe is a family favorite.

> 6 bratwurst sausages (about 1 pound total weight)
> 1 8-ounce can sauerkraut, drained
> 1 cup beer
> 1 teaspoon caraway seeds
> 6 crisp hard rolls or buns, split and toasted
> Coarse Horseradish Mustard (page 175)

1. In a frying pan, brown the sausages on all sides over medium heat.
2. Add the sauerkraut, beer, and caraway seeds. Cover and simmer for 30 minutes.
3. Serve the sausages and seasoned sauerkraut on the toasted rolls. Pass the mustard at the table.

YIELD: 6 servings.

Pizza Burgers

Pork sausage makes this burger unique and flavorful.

> 1 pound lean seasoned bulk pork sausage
> 1 4-ounce can sliced mushrooms, drained
> Canned pizza sauce
> 4 slices mozzarella cheese
> 4 Italian hard rolls, split and toasted, if desired

1. Shape the sausage meat into 4 patties. In a frying pan, brown the patties over medium heat until well done.
2. Spoon the mushrooms and 1 tablespoon of sauce over each patty. Top with a slice of cheese. Cover the pan and cook until the cheese melts, about 2 to 3 minutes. Serve on the split buns.

YIELD: 4 servings.

Italian Sausage Sandwich

This sandwich is easily prepared for one or many. In fact, if you're serving a crowd, the sausages can be prepared ahead and reheated when needed.

> *2 sweet or hot Italian sausage links*
> *¼ cup water*
> *1 tablespoon olive oil*
> *1 sweet green pepper, seeded and cut into 1-inch*
>   *strips*
> *2 hard rolls, split, or 4 slices Italian or French bread*

1. Put the sausages and water in a frying pan. Cover and simmer for 5 minutes. Pour off the water.
2. Add the oil and green pepper to the pan and sauté over medium-low heat until the sausages are browned and the peppers are soft, about 20 minutes.
3. To serve, put the peppers and sausages on rolls or bread.

YIELD: 2 servings.

Turkey Melt

Muenster cheese and dill pickles are the secret ingredients in this grilled sandwich.

> *4 slices rye bread*
> *Dijon mustard to taste*
> *Mayonnaise to taste*
> *4 slices Muenster cheese*
> *1 medium-size ripe tomato, sliced*
> *½ cup sliced dill pickles*
> *4 ounces cooked turkey breast, sliced*
> *Butter or margarine, softened*

1. Spread 2 slices of the bread with mustard and 2 with mayonnaise in the desired amounts.
2. On the bread with the mustard, assemble the sandwiches by equally dividing the cheese, tomato slices, pickles, and turkey. Top with the bread with the mayonnaise.

3. Butter the outsides of the bread slices and grill the sandwiches in a frying pan until golden on both sides.

YIELD: 2 servings.

Turkey-Avocado Pitas

This hot sandwich contains all the ingredients in your favorite chef's salad.

> *1¼ pounds fresh raw turkey breast, sliced (about 8 slices)*
> *½ cup bottled Italian salad dressing*
> *4 slices bacon*
> *8 slices swiss cheese*
> *2 whole wheat or white pita (pocket) breads, halved*
> *2 tablespoons mayonnaise*
> *1 medium-size ripe avocado, sliced*
> *1 medium-size ripe tomato, sliced*

1. Marinate the turkey slices in the salad dressing for 20 minutes.
2. In a frying pan, fry the bacon until crisp. Remove to paper towels to drain.
3. Sauté the turkey in bacon drippings until done, about 2 minutes on each side.
4. Top each turkey slice with a slice of cheese. Cook until the cheese melts.
5. Spread mayonnaise inside each pita bread. Place 2 slices of turkey in each half. Add the avocado and tomato slices. Top each serving with a bacon slice.

YIELD: 4 servings.

Western Sandwich

Sometimes known as the Denver Sandwich, this is the kind of meal that's good at any time of the day.

> 2 tablespoons butter or margarine
> ½ cup diced cooked ham
> ¼ medium sweet green pepper, diced
> ½ small onion, diced
> 3 large eggs
> 1 tablespoon milk
> ¼ teaspoon salt
> 4 slices white or whole wheat bread, toasted

1. In a frying pan, melt the butter over medium heat. Sauté the ham, green pepper, and onion until tender.
2. Meanwhile, in a mixing bowl, beat the eggs, milk, and salt together. Pour into the skillet. Turn the heat to low, cover, and cook until the eggs are set and lightly browned on the bottom.
3. Cut the omelet in half and serve each portion between the toasted bread slices.

YIELD: 2 servings.

Herbed Croque Monsieur

Ham, cheese, and turkey makes this sandwich satisfying; the batter adds uniqueness.

> 2 large eggs
> ½ cup milk
> ¼ teaspoon dried oregano
> ¼ teaspoon dried basil
> 8 slices white, whole wheat, Italian, or French bread
> Dijon mustard
> 4 slices fontina cheese
> 4 slices cooked ham
> 4 slices cooked turkey breast
> ¼ cup butter or margarine

1. In a mixing bowl, beat the eggs, milk, and seasonings together until well blended.
2. Assemble the sandwiches by spreading 4 bread slices with mustard. Divide the cheese, ham, and turkey evenly over the bread. Top with the remaining 4 slices of bread.

3. In a frying pan or griddle, melt the butter over medium-high heat.
4. Dip the sandwiches in the batter, letting any excess batter drain off. Brown the sandwiches on both sides. Serve immediately.

YIELD: 4 servings.

Grilled Mozzarella and Tomato Sandwich

This is a nice change from the traditional grilled cheese and tomato sandwich. It's elegant enough to serve to guests for lunch. Add a light soup or salad and a semidry white wine to complete the meal.

> *2 slices whole wheat bread*
> *2 slices mozzarella cheese*
> *2 slices ripe tomato*
> *Pinch of dried basil, or 1 teaspoon minced fresh basil*
> *Butter or margarine*

1. Preheat a griddle or frying pan over medium heat.
2. Assemble the sandwich by layering the cheese and tomato slices on 1 slice of bread. Sprinkle with the basil and top with the remaining slice of bread.
3. Spread butter on the outside of both slices of bread and grill until golden brown on both sides.

YIELD: 1 serving.

Chili Cheese-Wiches

This is a south-of-the-border version of the basic grilled cheese sandwich.

> *2 slices Monterey Jack cheese*
> *2 slices white bread*
> *Diced hot chiles to taste*
> *2 slices ripe tomato*
> *Butter or margarine*
> *Bottled salsa, optional*

1. Place a slice of cheese on 1 slice of bread. Add the chiles, tomato slices, and remaining cheese slice. Top with the remaining slice of bread.
2. Spread butter on the outside of both slices of bread.
3. Preheat a frying pan or griddle over medium heat. Grill the sandwich until golden brown on both sides.
4. Serve with the salsa, if desired.

YIELD: 1 serving.

Beer and Cheese Rarebit

Try this piquant sauce on toast and experience one of the most famous open-faced sandwiches. Serve with a crisp garden salad and a bottle of fruity white wine.

1 pound sharp Cheddar cheese, shredded
2 tablespoons butter or margarine
1/2 cup flat beer
1 tablespoon Dijon mustard
1 teaspoon Worcestershire sauce
1/2 teaspoon paprika
1 large egg, beaten
8 slices white bread, toasted and cut in half diagonally

1. In a saucepan, melt the cheese and butter over low heat. Cook and stir until smooth. Stir in the beer slowly. Then add the seasonings.
2. Quickly stir in the egg. Cook and stir until thickened. Serve over the toast points.

YIELD: 4 to 6 servings.

Garden Sandwich

Instead of serving a salad, why not prepare a sandwich with all the same healthy fix'n's?

4 slices whole wheat bread
1 small zucchini, shredded
4 slices ripe tomato
2 thin slices red onion
½ cup alfalfa sprouts
4 slices low-fat mozzarella cheese
Butter or margarine

1. Preheat a griddle or frying pan over medium heat.
2. Assemble the sandwich by dividing the vegetables and cheese evenly over 2 slices of bread. Top with the remaining bread.
3. Spread butter on the outside of each slice of bread and grill until golden brown on both sides.

YIELD: 2 servings.

SUGGESTED
SANDWICH MENUS

· *COLLEGE REUNION LUNCHEON* ·
Shrimp Curry Bisque (page 54)
Grilled Mozzarella and Tomato Sandwiches (page 46)
Kahlua Custard (page 193)
Beverage

· *SATURDAY AFTERNOON LUNCH WITH THE KIDS* ·
Tomato-Rice Soup (page 53)
Chili Cheese-Wiches (page 46)
Carrot and Celery Sticks
Fudge Brownie Wedges (page 197)
Beverage

· *HOT SUMMER'S EVE DINNER* ·
Garden Salad / Yogurt-Herb Dressing (page 170)
Italian Sausage Sandwiches (page 43)
Ice Cream with Mocha-Fudge Sauce (page 204)
Beverage

· *AFTER WORK SUPPER* ·
Tomato-Rice Soup (page 53)
Gourmet Hamburgers (page 38)
Fruit Garnish
Peanut Butter Chewies (page 199)
Beverage

· *LIGHT SUPPER AFTER THE THEATER* ·
Light White Wine
Minestrone with Italian Sausages (page 98)
Mixed Green Salad
Beer and Cheese Rarebit (page 47)
Poached Pears in Cognac (page 185)
Beverage

· *AFTER BIKING OR HIKING MEAL* ·
Herbed Croque Monsieur (page 45)
Assorted Relishes
Marinated Melon (page 188)
Beverage

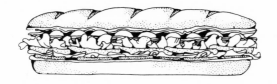

4
Tin-Can Canteen
Instant Meals on the Road or at Home

Do you often take to the road, with a few worldly possessions, for several days to "get away from it all"? If you do, you already know that half the fun of such trips is eating hearty home-cooked meals after working up an enormous appetite in the fresh air. Whether you're cooking over a campfire, a single burner, or a small range in a cabin or motel room, planning the menus is an all-important step before you can head for the hills!

The recipes in this chapter use a wide variety of packaged convenience foods to make cooking on the road a simple, enjoyable task. These packaged "helpers"are invaluable to the camper whose cooking space, refrigeration, and cleanup facilities are at a premium. Plan to tote a variety of canned, condensed, and packaged foods that can be mixed creatively to produce real meals, without a hassle. These recipes will teach you to create culinary works of art using a minimum of fresh ingredients.

But don't save this chapter for camping trips alone. Use it as a helper for the busy days when a quick meal at home is in order. Everyone needs a repertoire of "dump and heat" recipes. This chapter is dedicated to those times when an instant meal is needed, whether you're on the road or in town trying to keep the home fires burning.

Tips for Cooking on the Road

If you're planning a trip that requires cooking on the single burner on the road, here are a few hints that might be helpful:

- First and foremost, remember to keep the entire process simple. That goes for the equipment as well as the menu.

- Sit down with a pen and paper and plan how many meals and snacks are needed during the trip and in what quantities. Having enough food is important, but overkill is only going to get in the way.

- If you're going to be in a location where additional groceries can be purchased you may pack lighter, buying perishables and emergency items on the road. Research this before you complete the planning process so you can shop with confidence.

- Before planning the menu, address the amount of cooler or refrigerator space available. If this trip is, indeed, primitive, you'll select menus that consist totally of convenience foods and you'll pack the can opener. Stay away from perishables.

- Gather cooking utensils and purchase any basics that might be needed. Keep travel light and practical. You'll have little space in the car, the trailer, and at the final destination. Try to pack multipurpose items to save space.

- Don't forget to pack several rolls of aluminum foil. The heavy duty varieties are more versatile. Foil can be used as a frying pan, storage vessel, reflective oven, pot or pan cover, and more.

- Save coffee cans to use as cooking vessels. Some of the best one pot—one burner meals have been cooked in a 2- to 3-pound can. The best news is that they can be disposable if desired! Speaking of versatility, a coffee can will double as a rolling pin.

- Pack utensils and food in the order in which they will be used. This helps save time and effort later in small areas.

- If you're backpacking, plan to carry dehydrated foods and aluminum foil (take it off the roll and fold it around a flat piece of cardboard). Make a cooking vessel from the foil, add water to the dried meal, and cook over an open fire.

- Premeasure dry ingredients and place in small plastic bags with resealable tops. This is handy for flour breading mixtures for pan fried fish, for example.

- Pancakes can be a welcome hearty treat. Carry one of the many good box mixes with you. These mixes can also be used to prepare biscuits, dumplings, quick breads, pizza crusts, and more.

· Use dry milk for all milk needs.
· Canned chow mein noodles are a great way to have an instant crunchy bed for creamed dishes without cooking rice or noodles.

How to Use This Chapter at Home

· Plan ahead for those busy days. Buy and store enough ingredients to be able to prepare several of the recipes in this chapter at a moment's notice.
· Have the pages for those recipes marked so that any family member can prepare them when necessary. This is a nice insurance policy for you if you're delayed at the office.
· Do experiment with variations to these convenience recipes. Make them your own by adding special touches of herbs, your favorite vegetables, different soups and broths, or whatever strikes your fancy.
· Watch the grocery stores and newspapers for new food items that could add flavor and convenience to your diet.
· If sodium is a concern to you, read packages and canned goods labels for the levels they contain. Today there are many more prepared food choices with reduced- or no-sodium levels.
· Always begin planning a meal with the entrée. For additional "go-alongs," check the *Side-Dish Showstoppers* chapter (page 162) and *Desserts, Sweets, and Munchies* (page 179).
· Do let youngsters use this chapter for a way to become interested in the world of the culinary arts.

Spinach-Potato Soup

This is a perfect soup to pour into an insulated thermos and tote to a football game on a chilly day.

> 1 10-ounce package frozen chopped spinach, thawed and
>   well drained
> 1 10¾-ounce can chicken broth

3 cups milk
1 cup instant mashed potato flakes
1 tablespoon dehydrated instant chopped onion
1 4-ounce package shredded Cheddar cheese
1 cup cooked cubed ham

Combine all the ingredients in a large saucepan. Heat over medium heat until the mixture thickens and the cheese melts, about 10 minutes.

YIELD: 6 servings.

Tomato-Rice Soup

Keep a can of Italian tomatoes on hand and you have the basis for a quick but very delicious soup.

1 tablespoon butter or margarine
2 garlic cloves, minced
1 28-ounce can Italian tomatoes with liquid,
    puréed in a blender
1 teaspoon dried dill
1/2 teaspoon dried basil
Salt to taste
Freshly ground black pepper to taste
1/4 teaspoon sugar
2/3 cup long-grain rice
1 cup heavy cream
1 cup milk
Soup and Salad Croutons (page 173)

1. In a saucepan, melt the butter over medium-high heat. Sauté the garlic until it is lightly browned.
2. Stir in the puréed tomatoes, seasonings, sugar, and rice. Cover and cook over low heat until the rice is tender, about 15 to 20 minutes.
3. Stir in the cream and milk and heat through. Serve garnished with the croutons.

YIELD: 4 to 6 servings.

Quick Vegetarian Vegetable Soup

This soup is ready in less than 30 minutes. Meat can be added, if desired. In fact, this is a great place to use leftover pieces of cooked beef.

2 tablespoons vegetable oil
1 garlic clove, minced
1 medium-size onion, chopped
8 cups canned chicken broth
1 16-ounce can tomatoes with liquid, chopped
2 16-ounce packages frozen mixed vegetables, or any combination
 of your favorites
¼ cup alphabet pasta
1 teaspoon dried basil
Salt and freshly ground black pepper to taste
Grated Parmesan cheese

1. In a Dutch oven, heat the oil over medium heat. Sauté the garlic and onion until the onion is soft.
2. Add the chicken broth, tomatoes, frozen vegetables, pasta, and seasonings. Cover and cook until the pasta is soft and the vegetables are tender, about 15 minutes.
3. Serve with grated Parmesan cheese as a garnish.

YIELD: 12 servings.

NOTE: Freeze leftovers in individual serving portions for use at a later date.

Shrimp Curry Bisque

This delicate soup is perfect as a first course or hearty enough for a main dish when served in a bowl with French bread.

1 pound carrots, peeled and sliced into 1-inch pieces
1 medium-size onion, quartered
1 garlic clove
4 cups canned chicken broth
1 cup half-and-half
1 to 2 teaspoons curry powder
1 4½-ounce can small shrimp, well drained
Chopped fresh parsley leaves

1. Put the carrots, onion, garlic, and chicken broth into a sauce-pan. Cook, covered, over medium heat until the vegetables are very tender.
2. In a blender or food processor, purée the mixture until smooth. Pass the mixture through a fine sieve and return it to the saucepan. Heat over low heat. Stir in the half-and-half, curry powder, and shrimp. Heat through and serve with a garnish of chopped parsley.

YIELD: 4 servings.

Easy Taco Salad

There's no need even to brown ground beef with this easy version of the taco salad.

> *1 15-ounce can chili with or without beans*
> *1 head iceberg lettuce, shredded*
> *Diced ripe tomatoes*
> *Shredded Cheddar cheese*
> *Sour cream*
> *Frozen guacamole dip, thawed*
> *Corn chips*

1. In a saucepan, heat the chili to serving temperature.
2. Meanwhile, arrange the lettuce in salad bowls. Spoon the hot chili over the lettuce and top with the tomatoes, cheese, sour cream, and guacamole.
3. Garnish the outer edge of each salad bowl with corn chips.

YIELD: 2 to 3 servings.

Zesty Pizza Salad

This version of the taco salad can contain all the delicious in-gredients of your favorite pizza. Be selectively creative just as though you are going out for pizza! These are my choices. What are yours?

4 sweet or hot Italian sausage links, cut into ¹/₂-inch pieces
1 8-ounce can pizza sauce
1 4-ounce can sliced mushrooms, drained
1 head iceberg lettuce, shredded
¹/₂ cup sliced ripe (black) olives
¹/₄ cup chopped sweet green pepper
1 4-ounce package shredded mozzarella cheese
Packaged cheese croutons

1. In a frying pan, cook the sausages until well done. Drain off any excess fat. Add the sauce and mushrooms and heat through.
2. Meanwhile, arrange lettuce in 4 salad bowls. Top with olives, green pepper, and half of the cheese. Toss.
3. Top with the hot sausage mixture and garnish with the remaining cheese and croutons.

YIELD: 4 servings.

Camper's Stew

This is truly a one-burner, one-pot meal: Each serving is cooked in and eaten from a 2-pound coffee can. If the can is no longer needed, discard it.

1 pound lean ground beef
2 large potatoes, sliced
1 17-ounce can whole kernel corn, drained
1 15-ounce can stewed tomatoes
Salt and freshly ground black pepper to taste
1 cup biscuit mix
¹/₄ cup plus 2 tablespoons milk

1. Shape the meat into 4 patties to fit in the bottom of four 2-pound coffee cans. Grease all 4 cans and add the beef patties.
2. Top each patty with an equal amount of corn, potatoes, and tomatoes and season with salt and pepper.
3. Cover each can tightly with heavy duty aluminum foil. Grill 3 to 4 inches from the coals for 30 minutes.
4. Combine biscuit mix and milk with a fork. Remove the foil lids from the cans and drop the batter by spoonfuls into each can.

5. Cook, uncovered, for 10 minutes; then cover and cook for 10 minutes longer.

YIELD: 4 servings.

Beef and Noodle Platter

This dish is arranged as a work of art on a large serving platter. Don't worry, it's easy to do.

> 1 12-ounce package wide egg noodles
> 2 pounds lean ground beef
> 2 large onions, chopped
> 2 10¾-ounce cans tomato soup
> 1 4-ounce jar button mushrooms, drained
> 1 sweet green pepper, minced
> 1 16-ounce can chow mein noodles

1. Cook the egg noodles according to package directions. Drain and hold in a colander.
2. In a frying pan, brown the beef and onions over medium heat. Drain off any excess fat. Add the soup, cover, and simmer until thick, about 1 hour.
3. Add the mushrooms and heat through.
4. Warm the noodles in the colander with hot tap water; then drain well. Arrange on a platter. Top with the meat mixture, allowing an edge of noodles to peek through. Sprinkle with the green pepper. Make a border between the meat and egg noodles with the chow mein noodles.

YIELD: 8 servings.

Spanish Rice

This skillet dish is a meal that needs only a salad to complete it.

> *1 pound lean ground beef*
> *1 small onion, chopped*
> *1/2 sweet green pepper, chopped*
> *1 15-ounce can tomato sauce with herbs*
> *1 cup quick-cooking rice*
> *1 bay leaf*
> *1/2 teaspoon dried thyme*
> *Salt to taste*
> *Pinch of freshly ground black pepper*

1. In a frying pan, brown the beef, onion, and green pepper over medium heat. Drain off any excess fat.
2. Add the remaining ingredients, cover, and simmer for 20 minutes. Discard the bay leaf before serving.

YIELD: 4 servings.

Chimichangas

This is a popular dish in Mexican restaurants. It can easily be prepared at home using convenience foods.

> *1 pound lean ground beef*
> *1 medium-size onion, chopped*
> *1 garlic clove, minced*
> *1 11¼-ounce can chili beef soup*
> *1 4-ounce can chopped green chiles, drained*
> *1 teaspoon dried basil*
> *1/2 teaspoon ground cumin*
> *8 8-inch flour tortillas*
> *1 4-ounce package shredded Cheddar cheese*
> *Vegetable oil*
> *Shredded lettuce*
> *Sour cream*

1. In a frying pan, brown the beef, onion, and garlic over medium heat. Drain off any excess fat.
2. Add the soup, chiles, and seasonings. Cover and simmer for 10 minutes. Cool.
3. Spoon ¼ cup of the meat mixture onto the center of each tortilla. Top each with 1½ tablespoons of the cheese. Fold the tortillas envelope style and secure with a toothpick.

4. In a clean frying pan, heat 1 inch of oil to 375 degrees.
5. Fry two Chimichangas at a time and drain on paper towels. Then sprinkle with some of the remaining cheese. Repeat until all are fried.
6. Remove the toothpicks and put the Chimichangas on a bed of shredded lettuce. Serve garnished with a dollop of sour cream.

YIELD: 8 servings.

Grab-a-Mug Meal

This is a perfect hot meal for a cold winter evening. Serve a slice of French bread and a little fruit with this hearty dish.

> *1 pound lean grond beef*
> *1 cup elbow macaroni*
> *1 1½-ounce package chili seasoning mix*
> *1 16-ounce can whole tomatoes with liquid, broken up*
> *1 16-ounce can chili beans in gravy*
> *2 cups water*

1. In a saucepan, brown the beef over medium heat. Drain off any excess fat.
2. Add all the remaining ingredients and mix well. Bring to a boil and simmer until the macaroni is tender. Serve in your favorite large mug.

YIELD: 6 servings.

Convenience Stroganoff

This is a fast dinner for every day or gourmet for company, if you add a bottle of red wine to your menu. Serve the stroganoff over hot cooked noodles.

> *2 tablespoons butter or margarine*
> *1 pound boneless beef sirloin or round steak, sliced thin*
> *1 4-ounce can or jar button mushrooms, drained*
> *1 cup water*
> *½ envelope onion soup mix*
> *2 tablespoons all-purpose flour*
> *⅓ cup sour cream*

1. In a frying pan, melt the butter over medium heat. Sauté the beef slices and mushrooms until the beef is browned.
2. Add the water and soup mix, cover, and simmer until the beef is tender, about 30 minutes.
3. Combine the flour and sour cream. Add it to the beef mixture. Cook and stir until thickened, about 5 minutes.

YIELD: 4 servings.

No-Fuss Pot Roast

This classic convenience roast makes its own gravy and cooks the vegetables all in the skillet or Dutch oven. Because this recipe requires 2 hours to cook, save it for a weekend or cook it the night before and simply reheat after work.

> *1 tablespoon vegetable oil*
> *1 3-pound pot roast*
> *1 10¾-ounce can cream of mushroom soup, undiluted*
> *½ envelope onion soup mix*
> *½ cup water*
> *1 16-ounce package frozen stew vegetables*

1. In a skillet or Dutch oven, heat the oil over medium-high heat. Brown the meat on all sides.
2. Add the canned soup, soup mix, and water. Cover and simmer until the meat is tender, about 1½ hours.
3. Add the frozen vegetables, cover, and cook for 20 minutes.
4. Remove the meat and vegetables from the pan. Slice the meat and serve it with the vegetables and pan juices.

YIELD: 8 servings.

Chili-Mac

You'll like this recipe's simplicity; even the macaroni is cooked right in the skillet along with the rest of the ingredients. It is a perfect entrée for a camping trip.

> ½ *pound lean seasoned bulk pork sausage*
> ½ *sweet green pepper, diced*
> 1 *small onion, chopped*
> 1 *8-ounce can tomato sauce*
> ½ *cup elbow macaroni*
> ½ *teaspoon chili powder*
> ⅓ *cup sour cream*

1. In a frying pan, brown the sausage over medium heat. Add the green pepper and onion and cook until the vegetables are tender. Drain off any excess fat.
2. Add the tomato sauce, macaroni, and chili powder. Cover and simmer until the macaroni is done, about 20 minutes.
3. Stir in the sour cream and heat through, but do not boil.

YIELD: 2 servings.

Cassoulet

Traditionally this French country dish requires hours to prepare. Using convenience foods, your cassoulet is ready to serve in 30 minutes.

> ¼ *pound bacon*
> 1 *pound seasoned bulk pork sausage*
> 1 *pound smoked sausage links, sliced*
> 1 *16-ounce can red kidney beans, drained*
> 1 *16-ounce can white Great Northern beans, drained*
> 1 *16-ounce can stewed tomatoes*
> 2 *carrots, peeled and sliced thin*
> 2 *celery stalks, sliced*
> 1 *garlic clove, minced*
> 1 *tablespoon chopped fresh parsley leaves*
> 1 *teaspoon dried basil*

1. In a Dutch oven, cook the bacon over medium heat until it is crisp. Remove to paper towels to drain. Chop when cool and set aside.
2. Sauté the sausage meat and sausage slices in the Dutch oven until brown. Drain off any excess fat.

3. Add all the remaining ingredients. Cover and simmer for 20 minutes. Serve in large soup bowls garnished with the chopped bacon.

YIELD: 8 servings.

NOTE: If desired, this recipe can be prepared using dried beans. Cook according to package directions; then proceed as directed above.

Lasagna Casserole

Lasagna is a wonderful meal, but time consuming to assemble and prepare. This casserole has all the flavor but practically none of the work.

> *8 ounces wide noodles*
> *1 pound lean seasoned bulk pork sausage*
> *1 medium-size onion, chopped*
> *1 15½-ounce jar pizza sauce*
> *1½ cups cream-style cottage cheese*
> *1 4-ounce can sliced mushrooms, drained*
> *¼ cup grated Parmesan cheese*
> *1 8-ounce package sliced mozzarella cheese*

1. Cook noodles until they are *al dente.* Drain and set aside.
2. In a frying pan, cook the sausage and onion over medium heat. Drain off any excess fat.
3. Stir in the pizza sauce, cottage cheese, mushrooms, Parmesan cheese, and cooked noodles. Arrange the mozzarella cheese on top.
4. Cover and cook over low heat for 5 minutes, or until the cheese has melted. Serve immediately.

YIELD: 6 servings.

Sauced Pork Chops

This recipe was developed for a single serving. It's perfect for the busy nights when time is short but a hot, home-cooked meal is just what the doctor ordered.

> *1 teaspoon vegetable oil*
> *1 to 2 loin pork chops, ½ inch thick*
> *1 envelope instant tomato Cup·a·Soup*
> *¾ cup water*
> *Pinch of freshly ground black pepper*
> *Pinch of dried thyme*
> *1 8-ounce can mixed vegetables, drained*

1. In a frying pan, heat the oil over medium heat. Brown the chops on both sides. Drain off any excess fat.
2. Add the soup mix, water, and seasonings. Cover and simmer until the chops are tender, about 30 minutes. Add the vegetables and heat through.

YIELD: 1 to 2 servings.

Chops and Rice

This one-pan dinner will delight the entire family. Serve it with a salad and the menu is complete. Use this recipe for an after-work time-saver that even the least experienced cook can prepare.

> *1 tablespoon butter or margarine*
> *4 ½-inch-thick pork chops*
> *1 small onion, chopped*
> *1 sweet green pepper, diced*
> *1 medium-size zucchini, trimmed and sliced*
> *1½ cups quick-cooking rice*
> *1 teaspoon salt*
> *Pinch of freshly ground black pepper*
> *1 15-ounce can tomato sauce with herbs*
> *¾ cup water*

1. In a frying pan, melt the butter over medium heat. Brown the chops on all sides. Remove the chops from the pan as they brown and set them aside on a plate.
2. Sauté the vegetables in the pan for 2 minutes. Add all the remaining ingredients and top with the chops.
3. Cover and cook over low heat until the chops are tender and the rice is done, about 30 to 45 minutes.

YIELD: 4 servings.

Sweet and Sour Ham

This recipe will satisfy a yen for that tangy taste of sweet and sour. Serve it with hot cooked rice.

> 2 cups cubed cooked ham
> 1 16-ounce can pineapple chunks, drained and juice reserved
> ½ cup bottled barbecue sauce
> ⅓ cup cold water
> 1 tablespoon cornstarch
> 1 sweet green pepper, chopped

1. In a frying pan, combine the ham, pineapple juice, and barbecue sauce. Cover and cook over medium heat for 10 minutes.
2. Combine the water and cornstarch and stir the mixture into the pan. Cook and stir until thickened. Add the green pepper and pineapple and heat through.

YIELD: 4 servings.

Chicken and Rice

To make this dish, all you need to purchase at the last minute is the chicken. Everything else can come from your cupboard.

> 2 tablespoons vegetable oil
> 1 3-pound frying chicken, cut into serving pieces
> 1 cup water
> 1 10¾-ounce can cream of mushroom soup, undiluted
> 1 envelope onion soup mix
> 1 cup long-grain rice

1. In a skillet, heat the oil over medium heat. Brown the chicken on all sides. Remove the chicken from the skillet as it browns. Set it aside on a plate.
2. Combine all the remaining ingredients in the skillet and top with the chicken. Cover and cook over low heat until all the liquid is absorbed, about 1 hour.

YIELD: 4 servings.

Brown Rice Skillet Dinner

Good nutrition is the word of the day. Brown rice is both nutritious and delicious when prepared this way. You can use any fish, meat, or poultry in this recipe with equally satisfying results.

> *2 tablespoons vegetable oil*
> *1 3-pound frying chicken, cut into serving pieces*
> *1 4-ounce can sliced mushrooms, drained*
> *1 medium-size onion, chopped*
> *1 garlic clove, minced*
> *1 cup brown rice*
> *1 10¾-ounce can cream of mushroom soup, undiluted*
> *1 15-ounce can tomato sauce with herbs*
> *½ cup water*

1. In a skillet, heat the oil over medium heat. Brown the chicken on all sides. Remove the chicken from the pan as it browns. Set it aside on a plate.
2. Sauté the mushrooms, onion, and garlic in the pan until the onion is soft.
3. Add the rice and all the remaining ingredients. Top with the chicken parts. Cover and simmer for 1 hour, or until the rice is tender. Uncover and let stand a few minutes before serving.

YIELD: 4 servings.

Quick Chicken Divan

The insecure cook can prepare this foolproof dinner for any occasion! Add a succulent salad and a bottle of wine to complete this classy meal.

> *1 10¾-ounce can cream of chicken soup, undiluted*
> *1 10¾-ounce can cream of mushroom soup, undiluted*
> *2 cups cubed cooked chicken*
> *1 10-ounce package frozen chopped broccoli, thawed*
> *1 2-ounce jar sliced red pimiento, drained*
> *4 to 6 prepared patty shells*

In a frying pan or saucepan, combine the soups, chicken, and broccoli and cook, stirring, over medium-low heat. When all the ingredients are hot, add the pimiento. Serve over prepared patty shells.

YIELD: 4 to 6 servings.

Turkey and Stuffing

Why wait for Thanksgiving for this American favorite? Now you can dine on turkey after work in less than 30 minutes. Serve it with canned cranberry sauce to complete the meal. The sliced raw turkey breast is available at the meat counter of your supermarket.

> 1 7½-ounce package sage and onion stuffing mix
> 1 large egg, beaten
> 1 tablespoon chopped fresh parsley leaves
> 1½ pounds fresh raw turkey breast, sliced (8 slices)
> 2 tablespoons butter or margarine
> 2 carrots, cut into matchsticks
> 2 zucchini, cut into matchsticks
> 1 10½-ounce can mushroom gravy

1. Prepare the stuffing mix according to the package directions. Add the egg and parsley and mix well.
2. Place ¼ cup of the stuffing on a turkey slice, roll it up and secure with a toothpick.
3. In a frying pan, melt the butter over medium heat. Brown the turkey rolls on all sides.
4. Add the vegetables and gravy to the pan, cover, and simmer for 15 minutes.

YIELD: 8 servings.

Fish and Chips

Add a little tartar sauce and some coleslaw that you prepare or buy from the deli, and you have a great meal. If camping, use this idea for the fresh catch you expect to land. Pack a can of shoestring potatoes to substitute for the French fries.

2 pounds fresh perch fillets
1 cup instant mashed potato flakes
¼ cup grated Parmesan cheese
2 large eggs
Oil for deep-fat frying
1½ pounds frozen French fries

1. Wash the fish and pat it dry with paper towels. Combine the potato flakes and cheese.
2. Beat the eggs. Dip the fish into egg and then into the potato flakes and cheese mixture. Set aside.
3. Add enough oil to a skillet to make a ½-inch depth. Heat the oil to 375 degrees over medium-high heat.
4. Fry the potatoes until they are crisp. Drain on paper towels and keep warm.
5. Fry the fish for 3 to 5 minutes, or until crisp and golden. Drain on paper towels and serve at once.

YIELD: 8 servings.

Salmon Patties

On a "no time to market day," take a can of salmon from the cupboard shelf and prepare a treat. Serve it with a green salad and a garnish of fresh fruit.

1 large egg, beaten
5 tablespoons dry bread crumbs
2 tablespoons fresh lemon juice
1 teaspoon dehydrated minced onion
1 teaspoon dehydrated parsley flakes
Pinch of freshly ground black pepper
1 7¾-ounce can salmon, boned and drained
3 tablespoons butter or margarine

1. In a mixing bowl, combine the egg, 2 tablespoons of the bread crumbs, lemon juice, onion, parsley, pepper, and salmon. Shape into 2 patties.
2. Dredge the patties in the remaining crumbs.
3. In a frying pan, melt the butter over medium heat. Brown the patties on both sides.

YIELD: 2 servings.

Spaghetti in Red Clam Sauce

Besides being easy to prepare, this recipe is low in calories and delicious, of course!

> *8 ounces spaghetti*
> *1 tablespoon olive oil*
> *½ cup chopped onion*
> *1 6-ounce can minced clams, drained and liquid reserved*
> *1 15½-ounce jar spaghetti sauce*
> *1 tablespoon chopped fresh parsley leaves*
> *½ teaspoon dried basil*
> *Pinch of freshly ground black pepper*

1. Cook the spaghetti until it is *al dente*. Drain in a colander and set aside.
2. In a frying pan, heat the oil over medium heat. Sauté the onion until it is tender.
3. Add the clams, sauce, ½ cup of clam juice, and seasonings. Cover and simmer for 15 minutes.
4. Run hot tap water over the spaghetti in the colander to warm it. Drain well and toss with the sauce.

YIELD: 4 servings.

Quick Cheese Fondue

This is a perfect recipe for the out-of-doors. Simply heat all the ingredients together in a frying pan or saucepan and you're ready to dip and enjoy.

> *1 11-ounce can Cheddar cheese soup, undiluted*
> *8 ounces Swiss cheese, shredded*
> *French bread cubes*
> *Frankfurters, cut into 1-inch chunks*

In a saucepan or skillet heat the soup and cheese over low heat until the cheese melts. Serve with bread cubes and frankfurter bites as dippers.

YIELD: 4 servings.

Pan Pizza

When I say pan pizza, I mean pizza cooked in one pan, on *one burner*. This skillet pizza is simple to prepare and is perfect for the kids to fix. Vary the ingredients to suit your taste, taking care to use only cooked meats in the filling.

PIZZA CRUST (see Note)

> 1 package active dry yeast (regular or fast-rising)
> 1 teaspoon sugar
> ¾ cup warm water (105 to 115 degrees)
> 2 cups all-purpose flour
> ½ teaspoon salt
> Vegetable oil
> 2 tablespoons yellow cornmeal

PIZZA SAUCE

> 1 8-ounce can tomato sauce
> 2 tablespoons tomato paste
> ¼ teaspoon sugar
> ½ teaspoon dried oregano
> ½ teaspoon dried basil
> Salt to taste
> Pinch of hot red pepper flakes, optional

TOPPING

> 4 ounces pepperoni, sliced
> 1 small sweet green pepper, chopped
> 1 4-ounce can sliced mushrooms, drained
> 8 ounces mozzarella cheese, sliced or shredded
> ¼ cup grated Parmesan cheese

1. In a small bowl, combine the yeast, sugar, and warm water. Let stand until the mixture foams.
2. In a mixing bowl, combine the flour, salt, and yeast mixture. Mix with a wooden spoon until thick; then knead until smooth and elastic. No need to allow this recipe to rise.
3. With a rolling pin, roll the dough out to fit a 10- to 12-inch skillet. Grease the pan with oil and sprinkle the pan with cornmeal.

4. Put the rolled dough into the pan. Cover and bake over low heat until the bottom of the crust is lightly browned, about 15 minutes.
5. With a spatula, flip the crust over in the pan like a giant pancake.
6. In a small bowl, combine tomato sauce, tomato paste, sugar, and seasonings. Spread the sauce over the crust. Top with the pepperoni slices, green pepper, and mushrooms, then with the sliced cheese. Sprinkle with the Parmesan cheese.
7. Cover and bake until the cheeses melt, about 15 minutes.
8. Slide the pizza onto a cutting board and let rest for 5 minutes. Slice into serving-size pieces.

YIELD: One 10- to 12-inch pizza.

NOTE: If desired, a box of hot roll mix can be used to make the crust.

TOPPING VARIATIONS

Sausage Pizza—Substitute 3 sweet or hot Italian sausage links for the pepperoni. Sauté the sausages until well done, slice, and place on top of the sauce.

Ratatouille Pizza—Spread 1½ cups well-drained Ratatouille and Sausage Casserole (page 115) over the crust and pizza sauce. Top with mozzarella and Parmesan cheese.

Potato Salad and Franks

This hearty weekday recipe is so easy that even the kids can prepare it and love it.

> *1 tablespoon butter or margarine*
> *6 frankfurters, sliced (about 1 pound total weight)*
> *1 5½-ounce package dry scalloped potatoes with onion*
> *3¼ cups lukewarm water*
> *¼ cup white vinegar*
> *2 teaspoons sugar*
> *½ cup sliced celery*
> *¼ cup chopped sweet green pepper*

1. In a frying pan, melt the butter over medium heat. Brown the frankfurters on all sides.
2. Add the scalloped potato mix and water, cover, and simmer for 15 minutes.
3. Add the remaining ingredients. Cover and simmer for 10 minutes, or until the potatoes are tender.

YIELD: 6 servings.

Chili-Bean Franks

Make this quickly for luncheon on a Saturday when the family's home and hungry.

> 2 tablespoons butter or margarine
> 1/4 cup chopped onion
> 2 teaspoons chili powder
> 1 16-ounce can pork and beans in tomato sauce
> 2 tablespoons diced green chiles, optional
> 6 frankfurters
> 6 frankfurter buns
> Shredded Cheddar cheese

1. In a saucepan, melt the butter over medium heat. Sauté the onion until it is tender.
2. Add the chili powder, beans, green chiles, and frankfurters and heat through.
3. Toast the buns. Fill each with a frankfurter and a generous spoonful of the bean mixture. Garnish with shredded Cheddar cheese.

YIELD: 6 servings.

Taco Bag Lunch

The corn chip bag is the disposable dish for this meal. Teens will adore this quick meal on the weekend.

1 15-ounce can chili
2 ³/₄-ounce bags corn chips
¼ cup shredded Cheddar cheese
Chopped onion
Shredded lettuce
Bottled salsa

1. In a saucepan, heat the chili over medium heat.
2. Cut open the entire long side of each corn chip bag.
3. Spoon the chili into the bags and top with the cheese, onion, and shredded lettuce. Pass the salsa and dispose of the bags when the meal is finished.

YIELD: 2 servings.

Banana Boats

Looking for an easy dessert to prepare over the hot coals? This classic campfire treat is easy to tote and prepare. Kids of all ages will enjoy this one.

Bananas
Semisweet chocolate chips
Marshmallows
Roasted cocktail peanuts

1. Slice three quarters of the way through a banana lengthwise with the peel left on. Spread the banana open and stuff with any or all of the remaining ingredients.
2. Wrap in aluminum foil and place directly on the hot coals for 10 minutes. Carefully rotate several times to cook through.
3. Open the foil and serve with a spoon.

YIELD: 1 serving.

SUGGESTED
COOKING AT HOME
TIN-CAN CANTEEN MENUS

· *A SAVORY WEEKEND DINNER* ·
Red Wine
Tossed Salad
No-Fuss Pot Roast (page 60)
Cooked Noodles
Beverage
Peach Melba Sundae (page 195)

· *KIDS' TURN TO COOK* ·
Chicken and Rice (page 64)
Spinach Salad
Ice Cream with Peanut Butter Ice Cream Sauce (page 203)
Beverage

· *BUSY DAY LIFESAVER* ·
Grab-a-Mug Meal (page 59)
French Bread
Fresh Fruit
Beverage

· *QUICK AFTER-WORK SUMMER COOLER* ·
Zesty Pizza Salad (page 55)
Marinated Melon (page 188)
Iced Tea

· *QUICK ITALIAN FIESTA* ·
Red Wine
Lasagna Casserole (page 62)
Garden Salad
Bread Sticks
Italian Ice
or
Espresso Mousse (page 194)
Beverage

· *FEAST FOR ONE* ·
Sauced Pork Chops (page 62)
Green Salad
Dinner Roll
Ice Cream with Mocha-Fudge Sauce (page 204)
Beverage

SUGGESTED
COOKING ON THE ROAD
TIN-CAN CANTEEN MENUS

· *THE SOPHISTICATED CAMPER* ·
Red Wine
Cassoulet (page 61)
Fresh or Canned Fruit
Campfire Coffee

· *DOWN HOME DINNER* ·
Potato Salad and Franks (page 70)
S'mores
Campfire Coffee

· *HEARTY CAMPFIRE FARE* ·
Spanish Rice (page 57)
No-Oven Bacon Corn Bread (page 174)
Banana Boats (page 72)
Campfire Coffee

· *ONE POT MEAL* ·
Camper's Stew (page 56)
Pound Cake
Campfire Coffee

· *CAMPERS' FONDUE PARTY* ·
Quick Cheese Fondue (page 68)
French Bread
Frankfurters
Fresh Fruit
Campfire Coffee

5
Light and Lean

Americans today are eating fresher, lighter, and simpler meals. Eating light doesn't necessarily mean that you're on a "diet," but it does mean trimming the unnecessary calories and cholesterol in a painless way.

The recipes in this chapter were designed and tested to conform to this new way of life. Most dishes here contain fewer than 400 calories per serving, and are fun, creative, and satisfying. Years ago, eating light meant cooking special concoctions for some family members while the others ate the standard fare. Now everyone can enjoy the healthier cuisine and the chef needs to dirty but one pot!

You'll love the variety of exciting recipes available to you, from Beef Burgundy Slimmer to Pasta with Fresh Tomato and Zucchini. There are more interesting and palate-pleasing choices today than the dry broiled fish and bland poached chicken of yesterday's low-calorie diet.

Good health to you!

Helpful Hints for Eating Light

· Always consult a doctor before beginning a weight-reduction or special diet program.
· Instead of serving rice with many recipes, shred iceberg lettuce as you would for tacos and use it as a bed for the entrée.
· Don't be afraid of cheese if you're eating light. Substitute the leaner processed cheeses in the recipes calling for cheese.
· Meatless meals can be a nice change of pace while watching your weight. Legumes, such as beans, peas, and lentils, can be an interesting low-calorie source of protein and are low in cholesterol.

· Use yogurt instead of sour cream in dips and sauces to save calories. Be careful, however, never to boil yogurt as it will break down if overheated. Cottage cheese also can be an excellent substitute for sour cream. Simply blend 1 cup of low-fat cottage cheese with 2 tablespoons of lemon juice and 2 tablespoons of milk until smooth in a food processor or blender.

· Cut down on your salt intake by using herbs to flavor foods.

· Use the low-calorie vegetable cooking sprays instead of butter or margarine when frying foods.

· Limit your intake of high-fat meats. Trim all visible fat and try to eat more poultry, fish, and veal. Remove the skin from poultry to eliminate the fat that is harbored beneath the surface.

· Do serve potatoes and pasta occasionally. Watch the amounts eaten and the calories in the toppings. Remember, calories do count!

· Serve a large salad before the entrée. This technique will curb your appetite with very low-calorie vegetables and prevent overeating of higher-calorie foods during the next course.

· Serve ripe juicy fruits in season for dessert. They will satisfy the urge for something sweet.

· Popcorn that has been prepared in a hot-air popper can serve as an excellent low-calorie snack.

· Steam fish and vegetables for a healthful, low-calorie meal that can be ready in 15 minutes—perfect for after work.

· Use relishes with dinner. Celery and carrot sticks, radishes, and cherry tomatoes are delicious fat-free nibble food.

· Foods that contain higher fiber content will give you that "full feeling" and add the needed bulk that is important to the entire digestive system.

· Combine an exercise program with your new eating routine to receive maximum benefits from your efforts.

New Wave Minestrone

This soup is a meatless whole meal and needs only a light salad and, perhaps, Italian breadsticks to make it complete.

      1 28-ounce can tomatoes, cut up
      2 carrots, peeled and diced
      2 celery stalks, sliced
      1 10½-ounce can condensed beef broth
      1 small onion, chopped
      1 garlic clove, minced
      2 bay leaves
      4 cups water
      1 teaspoon dried basil
      1 teaspoon dried thyme, crushed
      4 ounces spaghetti, broken into small pieces
      1 15-ounce can chick-peas (garbanzo beans), drained
      2 medium zucchini, trimmed and sliced
      Grated Parmesan cheese

1. In a Dutch oven, combine the first 10 ingredients and bring to a boil over high heat.
2. Add the spaghetti. Turn the heat to low, cover, and simmer for 15 minutes.
3. Add beans and zucchini. Cook for 10 minutes. Remove the bay leaves and serve with the grated Parmesan cheese.

YIELD: 4 to 6 servings.

Lentil Soup

This filling recipe contains fiber for good health and flavor for good dining. You can enjoy this soup for about 110 calories per serving!

      1 cup dried lentils, sorted and rinsed
      6 cups chicken broth
      1 garlic clove, minced
      1 medium-size onion, chopped
      2 carrots, peeled and diced
      ½ teaspoon dried marjoram
      Salt and freshly ground black pepper to taste
      Chopped fresh parsley leaves

1. In a large saucepan or Dutch oven, combine all the ingredients except the parsley and bring to a boil.

2. Cover and simmer until the lentils are tender, about 2 hours. Garnish each serving with chopped parsley.

YIELD: 6 servings.

Eggplant Salad

This is a version of the well-known dish ratatouille. This version can be used as a salad, as a low-calorie appetizer with slices of French bread, or as a side dish with your favorite entrée.

> *Vegetable cooking spray*
> *1 large onion, diced*
> *1 sweet green pepper, diced*
> *1 pound zucchini, trimmed and diced*
> *1 pound eggplant, peeled and diced*
> *2 pounds ripe tomatoes, diced*
> *2 to 4 garlic cloves, minced*
> *1 tablespoon dried basil*
> *1 teaspoon dried oregano*
> *2 tablespoons chopped fresh parsley leaves*
> *Salt and freshly ground black pepper to taste*
> *½ pound fresh mushrooms, sliced*

1. Coat a skillet or Dutch oven with vegetable cooking spray.
2. Combine all the ingredients in the pan and sauté over medium heat until the juices begin to form. Lower the heat, cover, and simmer for 30 to 45 minutes. The vegetables should be soft. Serve hot or cold.

YIELD: 6 servings as a salad or side dish; 12 servings as an appetizer.

Shrimp and Vegetable Salad

Plan ahead when a scorcher is predicted. Prepare this salad the night before while the weather is still cool. Prepreparation is a must for this recipe, because the flavors of this salad need time to blend. After a hot day at the office, simply reach into the refrigerator for this cool, delicious dinner.

2 carrots, peeled and sliced diagonally
1 small head cauliflower, broken into flowerets
1 10-ounce package frozen green beans, thawed
3/4 pound shrimp, cooked, shelled, and deveined
1 cup diagonally sliced celery
2 green onions (scallions), sliced
1/2 cup bottled reduced-calorie Italian salad dressing (6 to 36
  calories per tablespoon)
Lettuce leaves

1. On a rack in a skillet or saucepan, steam the carrots, cauliflower, and green beans until crisp-tender, about 3 to 4
   minutes. Cool.
2. In a mixing bowl, combine the cooked shrimp, vegetables,
   and salad dressing. Marinate in the refrigerator several hours
   or overnight. Stir occasionally.
3. Serve on lettuce leaves.

YIELD: 4 servings.

Mexican Scramble

Add a little spice to scrambled eggs with this recipe. Serve it
for brunch, lunch, or a quick supper.

6 large eggs, beaten
1/2 cup skim milk
1/2 cup shredded Cheddar cheese
1/4 teaspoon salt
Dash of hot pepper sauce
Vegetable cooking spray
1/4 cup diced green chiles
2 green onions (scallions), sliced
2 medium-size ripe tomatoes, peeled, seeded, and diced
Shredded lettuce
Warm soft flour tortillas
Bottled salsa

1. In a mixing bowl, combine the eggs, milk, cheese, salt, and
   hot pepper sauce.
2. Coat a frying pan with vegetable cooking spray and heat
   over medium heat. Sauté the chiles and onion.

3. Add the egg mixture to the pan and cook, without stirring, until the mixture begins to set on the bottom. Lift and fold the eggs, bringing the set eggs to the surface. Continue folding until the eggs are almost dry.
4. Add the tomatoes and heat through.
5. Place a bed of lettuce on a serving platter. Spoon the egg mixture over the lettuce and serve with warmed tortillas and salsa.

YIELD: 4 servings.

Beef Burgundy Slimmer

Planning ahead pays off when you hit a deadline day at the office. Beef Burgundy Slimmer reheats well and, as an added bonus, it contains fewer than 250 calories per serving. Serve with ½ cup of hot cooked noodles for each serving.

Vegetable cooking spray
¾ pound beef round steak or lean beef stew meat, cut into 1-inch cubes
1 bay leaf
Salt and freshly ground black pepper to taste
Pinch of dried thyme
1¾ cups water
2 medium-size potatoes, peeled and diced
4 carrots, peeled and sliced
½ cup sliced celery
1 medium-size onion, chopped
1 cup sliced fresh mushrooms
3 tablespoons all-purpose flour
⅓ cup dry red wine
Chopped fresh parsley leaves

1. Spray a Dutch oven with vegetable cooking spray. Brown the beef over medium heat.
2. Add the seasonings and 1½ cups of the water to the pan. Bring to a boil, cover, and simmer for 1½ hours. Remove the bay leaf.
3. Add the vegetables and simmer for 20 minutes.

4. Combine the remaining ¼ cup of water and the flour. Add slowly to the meat mixture. Cook until thickened and stir in the wine. Garnish each serving with chopped parsley.

YIELD: 4 servings.

Stuffed Cabbage Leaves

This dish is one of my favorites. I serve it with a mixed green salad for an easy meal.

> *1 medium-size head green cabbage*
> *1 pound lean ground chuck or ground round*
> *½ cup quick-cooking rice*
> *Salt and freshly ground black pepper to taste*
> *Pinch of ground nutmeg*
> *2 cups water*

1. Put the cabbage in a saucepan and cover it with water. Bring to a boil, lower the heat, and simmer for 3 to 4 minutes.
2. Remove the cabbage from the water. Carefully remove 6 whole outer leaves from the head. Cut the remainder of the cabbage into wedges.
3. Combine meat, rice, and seasonings. Shape into 6 balls. Wrap a cabbage leaf around each meatball and secure with toothpicks.
4. Put the cabbage rolls and cabbage wedges in a saucepan. Add the 2 cups of water. Cover and bring to a boil. Lower the heat and simmer for 30 minutes. Discard the toothpicks before serving.

YIELD: 6 servings.

VARIATION
Use an 8-ounce can of tomato sauce instead of the water to simmer the cabbage rolls. Add a small amount of water, if necessary. Serve with the sauce.

Zesty Pork Casserole

Yes, you may eat pork if you're watching your weight. Just be sure to use lean pork that has been trimmed of all visible fat.

> *Vegetable cooking spray*
> *3/4 pound pork tenderloin, cut into thin slices*
> *1 medium-size onion, chopped*
> *1 8-ounce can tomato sauce*
> *1/3 cup water*
> *1 to 2 teaspoons chili powder*
> *1 teaspoon Worcestershire sauce*
> *1/4 teaspoon salt and a pinch of cayenne pepper*
> *1 12-ounce can whole kernel corn, drained*
> *1 sweet green pepper, cut into strips*
> *1 2-ounce jar red pimiento strips, drained*
> *1/4 cup shredded Cheddar cheese*

1. Coat a frying pan with vegetable cooking spray. Brown the meat and onion over medium heat.
2. Combine the tomato sauce, water, and seasonings. Add to pan, cover, and simmer over low heat for 10 minutes.
3. Stir in the corn, green pepper, and pimiento strips. Simmer, uncovered, until the green pepper is tender, about 10 minutes.
4. Sprinkle with cheese before serving.

YIELD: 4 servings.

Chicken Breasts with Curried Apple

With fewer than 200 calories per serving, this spicy dish tastes like the high-calorie versions.

> *1 small apple, peeled and chopped*
> *1 green onion (scallion), sliced*
> *1 to 2 teaspoons curry powder*
> *1 garlic clove, minced*
> *Salt to taste*
> *3/4 cup water*
> *2 chicken breasts, skinned, boned, and halved*
> *1 4-ounce can sliced mushrooms, drained and 1/3 cup*
> *liquid reserved*
> *1 teaspoon cornstarch*

1. In a frying pan, combine the apple, onion, curry powder, garlic, salt, and water. Bring to a boil over high heat. Add the chicken and lower the heat. Cover and simmer for 20 to 25 minutes, or until the chicken is tender.
2. Remove the chicken to a platter and keep it warm.
3. Combine the ⅓ cup reserved mushroom liquid and corn-starch and stir the mixture into the cooking juices in the frying pan. Cook and stir over medium heat until the mixture bubbles and thickens. Add the mushrooms and heat through. Pour the sauce over the chicken and serve.

YIELD: 4 servings.

Poached Chicken Breasts with Broccoli Purée

If you're very serious about cutting calories, this recipe is the one for you. It's very low in fat and high in nutrition while being very gourmet. The dish is especially pretty if it is presented as described below.

> ½ *cup canned chicken broth*
> ½ *cup dry white wine*
> ½ *teaspoon dried thyme*
> ¼ *cup fresh lemon juice*
> 3 *chicken breasts, skinned, boned, and halved*
> 1 *pound fresh broccoli, thick stems removed*
> 1 *10-ounce package frozen peas*
> 1 *cup chopped celery*
> 1 *medium-size potato, peeled and cut into 1-inch cubes*
> 1 *garlic clove, minced*
> *Lemon slices, optional*

1. In a frying pan, bring the chicken broth, wine, thyme, and lemon juice to a boil. Lower the heat and add the chicken breasts, broccoli, peas, celery, and potato. Cover and simmer for 15 minutes.
2. When the vegetables are tender, remove them to a blender container with a slotted spoon. Allow the chicken to continue to cook while processing vegetables.
3. Ladle off ½ cup of the poaching liquid and pour it over the vegetables in the blender. Add the garlic, cover, and blend on high until smooth.

4. When the chicken breasts are cooked, spoon the vegetable purée onto each plate and top with a chicken breast. Garnish chicken with lemon slices, if desired.

YIELD: 6 servings.

Paella

This dish originated in Spain, but it has international appeal today. You may make it in a skillet or wok, a perfect pan for this dish! Believe it or not, this recipe has fewer than 350 calories per serving.

Vegetable cooking spray
1½ pounds chicken pieces
2 sweet or hot Italian sausage links, sliced ½ inch thick
1 medium-size onion, chopped
1 sweet green pepper, chopped
1 large ripe tomato, chopped
2 garlic cloves, minced
1 cup long-grain rice
2 cups canned chicken broth
¼ teaspoon saffron threads, crushed
1 10-ounce package frozen peas
½ pound fresh or frozen shrimp, shelled and deveined
12 mussels in shell, scrubbed and debearded
12 clams in shell, scrubbed
¼ pound low-fat cooked ham, cut into cubes

1. Heat a wok or a skillet over medium heat. Coat with vegetable cooking spray. Sauté the chicken until browned. Remove and set aside. Sauté the sausage pieces until browned. Drain off any excess fat.
2. Add the onion, green pepper, tomato, garlic, rice, chicken broth, saffron, and chicken to the pan. Bring to a boil, cover, and simmer for 25 to 30 minutes.
3. Add the peas, seafood, and ham. Cover and cook until the rice is tender and the seafood is done, about 15 minutes. The shrimp will turn pink and the clams and mussels will open. Discard any shells that do not open.

YIELD: 8 servings.

Turkey Tacos

Watching your weight but still hungry for the taste of your high-calorie favorites? Here's a guilt-free recipe for you!

> *1 8-ounce can stewed tomatoes*
> *1 package taco seasoning mix*
> *2 cups diced cooked turkey or chicken*
> *¼ cup diced sweet green pepper*
> *6 to 8 soft flour tortillas*
> *Shredded lettuce*
> *Shredded Cheddar cheese*
> *Diced ripe tomatoes*
> *Bottled salsa*

1. In a skillet, combine the stewed tomatoes, seasoning mix, turkey, and green pepper. Simmer until thickened, about 10 minutes.
2. Warm the tortillas according to the package directions.
3. Spoon the turkey mixture onto the tortillas and top with lettuce, cheese, and diced tomatoes. Fold the tortillas over the filling. Pass the salsa at the table.

YIELD: 6 servings.

Lean Shrimp Newburg

You'll love this trimmed-down version of the rich Seafood Newburg! If desired, tuna or crab meat may be substituted for the shrimp.

> *1 tablespoon butter or margarine*
> *2 tablespoons cornstarch*
> *1¼ cups skim milk*
> *2 large egg yolks, beaten*
> *½ pound shrimp, shelled, deveined, and cut in half lengthwise*
> *1 tablespoon dry sherry*
> *1 tablespoon fresh lemon juice*
> *Salt to taste*
> *2 English muffins, split and toasted*
> *Chopped fresh parsley leaves*

1. In a saucepan, melt the butter over medium heat. Stir in the cornstarch and immediately add the milk. Stir and cook until thickened.
2. Add half the milk mixture to the egg yolks, stirring constantly. Return to the saucepan. Cook and stir until bubbly.
3. Add the shrimp and cook and stir until the shrimp turns pink. Stir in the sherry, lemon juice, and salt.
4. Serve immediately over English muffin halves, garnished with the chopped fresh parsley.

YIELD: 4 servings.

Cioppino

This fish stew is a favorite on the West Coast, but you can prepare it no matter where you live, because the seafood in the dish is available anywhere. Serve it with French bread and a salad.

1 medium-size onion, chopped
1 sweet green pepper, chopped
⅓ cup packed fresh parsley leaves, chopped
2 to 4 garlic cloves, minced
½ cup canned chicken broth
1 16-ounce can tomatoes with liquid, chopped
1 bay leaf
¼ teaspoon dried thyme
¼ teaspoon dried marjoram
¼ teaspoon hot pepper sauce
Pinch of freshly ground black pepper
½ cup dry white wine
1 pound frozen halibut or cod, thawed and cut into 1-inch cubes
½ pound shrimp, shelled and deveined
½ pound scallops

1. In a saucepan or Dutch oven, bring onion, green pepper, parsley, garlic, chicken broth, tomatoes, and seasonings to a boil. Lower the heat, cover, and simmer for 20 minutes.
2. Add the wine and seafood and simmer for 10 minutes, or until done. Remove the bay leaf and serve the stew in a shallow soup bowl.

YIELD: 6 servings.

Slimmed-Down Bouillabaisse

This gourmet seafood chowder is elegant enough to serve as a company dish. The long list of ingredients may make it look complicated, but it's really simple to prepare and has fewer than 250 calories per serving.

1 pound fresh or frozen fish fillets, cut into 1-inch chunks
1 pound fresh or frozen shelled shrimp and/or crab meat (Cut the crab into chunks. See Note.)
1½-pound live lobster, or 2 ½-pound lobster tails
3 tablespoons vegetable oil
4 medium-size ripe tomatoes, peeled and diced
2 medium-size onions, chopped
2 tablespoons chopped fresh parsley leaves
2 garlic cloves, minced and 1 bay leaf
½ teaspoon dried thyme, crushed
½ teaspoon dried savory, crushed
¼ teaspoon saffron threads, crushed
¼ teaspoon fennel seeds, crushed
Salt and freshly ground black pepper to taste
3 cups water
2 pounds fresh clams or mussels in shell, scrubbed (see Note)
1 cup dry white wine

1. Thaw the fish and shrimp if they are frozen. Heat enough salted water in a Dutch oven to cover the lobster. Plunge the live lobster into the boiling water; lower the heat to a simmer, cover, and cook for about 10 minutes. The lobster tails should be simmered for only 5 to 7 minutes, or just until done.
2. Remove the lobster from the water and cut the tail and claws into serving-size pieces. Set aside.
3. In the Dutch oven, heat the oil over medium heat. Sauté the vegetables and garlic until soft.
4. Add the seasonings, water, fish, shrimp, and clams. Cover and bring to a boil. Simmer for 6 to 8 minutes, or until the fish is done.
5. Stir in the wine and lobster and heat through. Discard any clams or mussels that do not open.
6. Discard the bay leaf and serve the broth and seafood in large soup bowls.

YIELD: 10 servings.

NOTE: Substitute any combination of seafood, depending on your personal taste and availability.

Door County Fish Boil

In the northern peninsula of Wisconsin this is a summer favorite. Although it is generally cooked out of doors, this is a version that can be prepared at any time of the year at home.

> ½ *pound unpeeled small red potatoes*
> ½ *pound small carrots, peeled and cut into 2-inch pieces*
> *1 large onion, sliced thick*
> *Salt to taste*
> *1 bay leaf*
> *1 pound fresh or frozen fish steaks (whitefish, trout, etc.)*

1. Put the potatoes, carrots, onion, salt, and bay leaf in enough water to cover in a Dutch oven. Cook over medium heat until the vegetables are almost tender.
2. Add the fish, cover and simmer until the fish flakes when tested with a fork.
3. Remove the fish and vegetables from the liquid with a slotted spoon and serve immediately.

YIELD: 2 to 3 servings.

NOTE: This recipe can be prepared in quantity, if desired.

Steamed Fish Dinner

This one-dish meal can be ready in 15 minutes!

> *2 to 4 5-ounce salmon or halibut steaks,* ½ *inch thick*
> *Salt and freshly ground black pepper to taste*
> *Lemon slices*
> *1 to 2 medium-size zucchini, trimmed and sliced*
> *4 to 8 small red potatoes, halved*

1. Place a steaming rack or basket in a Dutch oven. Pour 2 inches of water into the pan.

2. Place the fish steaks on the rack and season with salt and pepper. Top with the lemon slices. Lay the vegetables next to the fish.
3. Cover the pan and bring to a boil. Steam the fish and vegetables until the vegetables are tender and the fish flakes easily when tested with a fork, about 15 minutes.

YIELD: 2 to 4 servings.

NOTE: You can substitute any of your favorite vegetables for the zucchini and potatoes.

Pasta with Fresh Tomato and Zucchini

For you live-aloners, here's a recipe for one. You may, however, prepare this dish in larger quantities if more than one person will be dining.

> *2 ounces pasta, any size or shape*
> *Vegetable cooking spray*
> *½ cup shredded zucchini*
> *1 large ripe tomato, peeled, seeded, and diced*
> *2 tablespoons chopped fresh parsley leaves*
> *1 garlic clove, minced*
> *Hot red pepper flakes to taste*
> *Salt and freshly ground black pepper to taste*
> *1 large egg yolk*
> *2 tablespoons grated Parmesan cheese*

1. In a saucepan, cook pasta until *al dente.* Drain and set aside.
2. Spray a saucepan with vegetable cooking spray. Sauté the zucchini, tomato, parsley, and garlic for 2 minutes. Season with the red pepper flakes and salt and pepper. Add the cooked pasta and toss.
3. Quickly add the egg yolk and toss to coat. Sprinkle with the grated cheese and serve immediately.

YIELD: 1 serving.

Skinny Spaghetti Skillet Supper

Stay slim and "sup" on spaghetti with this one-pot, one-burner recipe. Enjoy this dish for under 300 calories a serving.

> 1 pound lean ground beef or ground round
> 1 6-ounce can tomato paste
> 1 14½-ounce can whole tomatoes with liquid, chopped
> 1½ cups water
> 1 teaspoon dried oregano
> 1 teaspoon dried basil
> ½ teaspoon garlic powder
> 6 ounces spaghetti, broken into pieces
> Grated Parmesan cheese

1. In a frying pan, brown the meat over medium heat. Remove from the pan, draining off the excess fat.
2. Put the tomato paste, tomatoes with liquid, water, and seasonings into the frying pan. Bring to a boil, lower the heat, cover, and simmer for 30 minutes.
3. Add the browned meat and spaghetti. Cover and cook, stirring occasionally, until the spaghetti is tender, about 10 minutes. Serve with the grated cheese.

YIELD: 6 servings.

Steamed Carrot-Zucchini Cake

For just over 100 calories you can enjoy a serving of this moist cake at any time of the day, or you can serve it for dessert with any meal.

> ½ cup all-purpose flour
> ¼ teaspoon baking soda
> ¼ teaspoon baking powder
> ⅓ cup packed brown sugar
> Pinch of salt
> ½ teaspoon ground cinnamon
> ¼ teaspoon ground nutmeg
> 1 large egg
> 1 tablespoon butter or margarine, softened (continued)

½ cup finely shredded carrot
½ cup finely shredded zucchini
¼ teaspoon grated lemon rind
3 tablespoons unsalted sunflower seeds

1. Grease a 2½-cup ovenproof bowl or steamed pudding mold.
2. Combine the dry ingredients in a mixing bowl.
3. Beat the egg and butter together and stir into the dry ingredients. Mix well.
4. Add the remaining ingredients and mix well.
5. Pour the batter into the prepared bowl or mold. Cover tightly with aluminum foil. Place in a Dutch oven on a rack. Pour in hot water to reach halfway up the bowl or mold. Cover the Dutch oven and simmer for 1½ hours.
6. Remove the cake and cool it, still in the bowl or mold, on a wire rack until just warm. Unmold and serve warm or let cool completely. It's delicious either way.

YIELD: 6 to 8 servings.

Energy Cookies

Believe it or not, these cookies contain fewer than 45 calories each; so when you get that craving for something sweet, you don't have to ignore it—indulge!

½ cup packed brown sugar
½ cup creamy peanut butter
¼ cup evaporated milk
2½ cups crisp rice cereal

1. In a saucepan, combine the brown sugar, peanut butter, and milk over medium heat.
2. Bring to a boil and stir constantly until the mixture is smooth.
3. Remove from the heat and stir in the cereal.
4. Drop by teaspoonfuls onto wax paper. Remove from wax paper when cool. Refrigerate in an airtight container.

YIELD: 3 dozen cookies.

Apricot Fondue

This dessert is a no-bake, low-calorie apricot sauce, which uses pieces of fruit as dippers.

> *1 16-ounce can apricots packed in water*
> *1 teaspoon cornstarch*
> *¼ teaspoon ground cinnamon*
> *Pinch of ground allspice*
> *½ teaspoon vanilla extract*
> *1 apple, cut into wedges*
> *1 pint strawberries*
> *1 banana, cut into chunks*

1. In a blender container, combine the apricots with their juice, cornstarch, and spices. Cover and blend on medium-high speed until smooth.
2. Heat the apricot mixture in a fondue pot or small saucepan until thickened, stirring occasionally. Add the vanilla and keep warm over low heat.
3. Using fondue forks or bamboo skewers, serve the sauce with fruit dippers of apples, strawberries, and bananas.

YIELD: 4 servings.

Fruit Salad Mélange

A perfect ending to any light meal or a colorful beginning to a brunch!

> *1 20-ounce can pineapple chunks packed in natural juices, drained and liquid reserved*
> *1 11-ounce can mandarin oranges, drained and liquid reserved*
> *2 tablespoons cornstarch*
> *1 8-ounce container vanilla-flavored yogurt*
> *1 cup seedless green grapes, halved*
> *1 banana, sliced*
> *1 apple, cored and chopped*

1. In a saucepan, combine the pineapple liquid, orange liquid, and cornstarch. Heat, stirring constantly, until thickened. Cool.

2. Combine all the ingredients in a large bowl and chill for several hours before serving.

YIELD: 8 servings.

SUGGESTED
LIGHT AND LEAN MENUS

· *LIGHT DINNER FOR ONE* ·
Pasta with Fresh Tomato and Zucchini (page 90)
Garden Salad
Energy Cookies (page 92)
Beverage

· *HEALTHY COMPANY FARE* ·
White Wine Coolers
Slimmed-Down Bouillabaisse (page 88)
Mixed Green Salad
Light Italian Salad Dressing
French Bread
Apricot Fondue (page 93)
Beverage

· *FAMILY SLIMMER* ·
Steamed Fish Dinner (page 89)
Garden Salad
Reduced-Calorie French Dressing
Breadsticks
Steamed Carrot-Zucchini Cake (page 91)
Beverage

· *AFTERNOON LIGHT LUNCH* ·
Shrimp and Vegetable Salad (page 79)
Assorted Mini-Muffins
Fruit Salad Mélange (page 93)
Beverage

· *AFTER THE "RUN" DINNER* ·
Skinny Spaghetti Skillet Supper (page 91)
Tossed Salad
Reduced-Calorie Ranch Dressing
Thinly Sliced French Bread
Frozen Fruit Yogurt
Energy Cookies (page 92)
Beverage

6
Country Cooking

Remember the great meals that mom or grandmother used to make, using every kettle in the house? The aromas of soups, stews, and ethnic specialties filled the house as they simmered on the stove for hours. Mothers had that special knack of combining meats, vegetables, and seasonings to produce fine works of art in their kitchens. For the rest of the family members, there was a certain comforting feeling about coming home to these lovingly prepared hearty meals.

Today, small kitchens and tight time schedules don't always permit a four-burner production to bring one of these old-fashioned meals to the table. This chapter was developed for the purpose of streamlining some of the classic recipes to fit the life-styles of today and the convenience of the single burner.

Now you can enjoy stews that make their own gravy, quick sauerbraten, one-hour goulash, gumbos, and more. All of these are just as tenderly prepared as in years gone by, but all are prepared with the convenience of *one burner!*

Tips for Preparing Soups and Stews

For the most part, soups and stews must be prepared several hours ahead of serving time. Meats tenderize and flavors blend only through long, slow simmering over gentle heat. This simmering can be done on the weekend, when time is available, or during the evening before the meal is to be served. The overnight standing time allows the dish to develop a richer, more full-bodied flavor and allows the chef the convenience of simply reheating the meal a few minutes before serving.

- **Rich Soup Stock**—Take care to cook basic soup stock for hours to extract the maximum flavor from the meat and soup bones.

- **Eliminate Fat and Cholesterol**—If soups and stews are prepared ahead of serving they can be refrigerated to allow the fat to rise to the top and congeal. Before reheating remove the hardened fat to eliminate unnecessary calories and cholesterol.

- **Freezer Meals**—Soups and stews freeze well. Prepare as directed. Freeze in containers or save space by freezing in boilable freezer bags that are heat sealed. Store these bags flat in the freezer until ready to use; then defrost and reheat in boiling water or in the microwave oven. This concept is especially convenient for busy evenings after work. Even children can warm a meal that is ready and waiting in the freezer.

- **Soups and Stews Are Creative**—Be adventurous and vary the seasonings and vegetables used in your dish. Try to keep the proportions about the same as the original recipe, but let your imagination or personal tastes guide you to new combinations.

- **Dumplings**—Most soups and stews are complete meals, needing only a little crusty French bread or, in the case of stews, cooked noodles or biscuits. Drop dumplings are yet another option, for they can be added right to the soup or stew pot to complete the meal in a single pot, on the *one burner*. Try the Parsley Drop Dumplings (page 172) for stew and Egg Drop Dumplings (page 172) for soup. You'll love the convenience of these country-style recipes.

- **Croutons**—Soups can also be garnished with chunky, homemade croutons that are prepared with stale bread that might have been tossed out. Prepare them ahead and store them in an airtight container. See page 173 for recipe.

- **Sodium Watchers**—If you are watching your sodium intake, discover the use of herbs to season your recipes.

Hearty Vegetable Soup

This is my mother's recipe. I think you'll enjoy it. For a richer-flavored soup, substitute oxtails for the soup bones. I also like to add 2 to 3 tablespoons of Pesto Sauce to the completed soup,

to give it the taste of herbs and cheese that goes so well with
vegetable soup.

2½ pounds soup bones with meat remaining
10 cups water
1 cup celery leaves
1 small onion, halved
6 whole black peppercorns
2 bay leaves
1 tablespoon salt
1 cup quick-cooking barley
1 14½-ounce can whole tomatoes with liquid, diced
1 16-ounce package frozen mixed vegetables (see Note)
Chopped fresh parsley leaves, or 2 to 3 tablespoons Pesto Sauce
*   (page 168)*

1. In a Dutch oven, combine the soup bones, water, celery
   leaves, onion, and seasonings. Bring to a boil over high heat,
   cover, and simmer for 2 hours.
2. Discard the celery leaves, onion, peppercorns, and bay leaves.
   Remove the meat from the bones and dice the meat and set
   it aside.
3. Meanwhile, bring the stock to a boil. Add the barley, cover,
   and cook until it is tender, about 10 minutes.
4. Add the reserved meat, tomatoes, and mixed vegetables.
   Simmer until the vegetables are tender.
5. Serve garnished with chopped parsley, or stir in the Pesto
   Sauce.

YIELD: 10 to 12 servings.

NOTE: If desired, 1½ quarts of sliced and diced fresh vegetables
can be used. Select favorites such as sliced celery, diced carrot,
shredded cabbage, sliced zucchini, diced potato, cut green beans,
diced celery root, or diced rutabaga.

Minestrone with Italian Sausages

This is a quick soup that can make a whole meal when served
with French bread and a bottle of red wine.

3 tablespoons olive oil
1 pound sweet or hot Italian sausage links
1 large onion, sliced thin
4 carrots, peeled and sliced
1 sweet green pepper, diced
3 medium-size zucchini, diced
2 celery stalks, sliced
1 small head green cabbage, shredded
¾ pound fresh green beans, cut into 1-inch pieces,
or 1 9- to 10-ounce package frozen cut green beans
1 28-ounce can Italian plum tomatoes with liquid, chopped
4 cups canned beef broth
2 teaspoons dried oregano
1 teaspoon dried basil
1 teaspoon salt
¼ teaspoon freshly ground black pepper
1 12- to 16-ounce can cannellini, chick-peas, or Great Northern
beans, drained
¼ pound cheese-stuffed tortellini or shell-shape pasta
Grated Parmesan cheese

1. In a Dutch oven, heat the oil over medium heat. Brown the sausages on all sides; then remove, slice, and set aside.
2. In the sausage drippings, sauté the *fresh* vegetables until crisp-tender.
3. If using the frozen beans, add them at this point along with the tomatoes, beef broth, and seasonings. Cover and simmer over low heat for 1 hour.
4. Add the canned beans and tortellini, cover, and cook until the pasta is tender, about 20 minutes.
5. Add the cooked sausage slices and heat through. Serve in large soup bowls topped with the grated cheese.

YIELD: 8 servings.

Hearty German Bean Soup

Prepare this soup on a cold winter's night to warm the family when they come home. This is one of those rare soups with old-fashioned flavor that can be prepared in less than 30 minutes.

2 slices bacon, chopped
1 small onion, chopped
¼ cup chopped fresh parsley leaves
½ teaspoon dried marjoram
Pinch of freshly ground black pepper
2 15-ounce cans chicken broth
8 ounces smoked sausages, bratwurst, Polish sausages,
    or frankfurters, sliced
1 16-ounce package frozen mixed vegetables
1 16-ounce can white beans with liquid

1. In a saucepan, cook the bacon until it is crisp. Discard all but 1 tablespoon of fat from the pan.
2. Add the onion and sauté until tender.
3. Add all the remaining ingredients, cover, and simmer for 20 minutes.

YIELD: 6 servings.

Bacon and Pea Soup with Egg Drop Dumplings

This recipe uses bacon instead of the usual ham bone for real convenience. Complete the soup with Egg Drop Dumplings for a hearty, economical meal.

¼ pound bacon, diced
1 medium-size onion, diced
1 pound dried split peas, sorted and washed
8 cups water
2 carrots, peeled and diced
2 celery stalks, diced
1 bay leaf
¼ teaspoon dried marjoram, crushed
Salt and freshly ground black pepper to taste
Egg Drop Dumplings (page 172)

1. In a Dutch oven, sauté the bacon and onion over medium heat until the onion is soft. Drain off any excess fat.
2. Add all the remaining ingredients except the dumplings and bring to a boil. Cover and Simmer until the peas are soft, about 2 hours.

3. Bring the soup to a boil. Drop the prepared dumpling batter by teaspoonfuls into the soup. Cook for 5 minutes.

YIELD: 6 to 8 servings.

Chicken, Noodle, and Vegetable Soup

Over the years, this recipe has been used as a remedy to cure the common cold. Whether it has magic healing qualities or not, this recipe is indeed a cure for the craving we all have, from time to time, for a good cup or bowl of homemade soup. Serve with a salad, rolls, and cheese.

> *5 pounds chicken parts*
> *3 quarts water*
> *1 leek, well cleaned*
> *1 carrot, peeled*
> *2 cups celery tops*
> *Salt*
> *10 whole black peppercorns*
> *1 cup peeled and diced carrot*
> *1 cup sliced celery*
> *4 ounces fine egg noodles*
> *Chopped fresh parsley leaves*

1. Put the chicken, water, leek, carrot, celery tops, 1 tablespoon of salt, and peppercorns into a Dutch oven. Bring to a boil and skim off any foam that floats to the top. Cover and simmer for 2 hours.
2. Remove the chicken with a slotted spoon and set it aside on a plate. Skim the fat and remove and discard the vegetables and peppercorns. (At this point, the soup and chicken can be covered and refrigerated until the following day, if desired. The fat will be easier to remove after chilling.)
3. Remove the meat from the chicken bones and dice it. Discard the skin and bones. Bring the stock to a boil and add the diced chicken and vegetables. Cook until the vegetables are tender.
4. Add the noodles and boil until done, about 5 minutes. Adjust the seasonings and serve in soup bowls. Sprinkle each serving with chopped parsley.

YIELD: 8 servings.

NOTE: Egg Drop Dumplings (page 172) can be substituted for the noodles, if desired.

New England Clam Chowder

This hearty, whole-meal soup will soon become a family favorite.

> *2 tablespoons butter or margarine*
> *1 small onion, chopped*
> *1 large potato, peeled and diced*
> *1 celery stalk, diced*
> *¼ cup all-purpose flour*
> *3 cups milk*
> *1 chicken bouillon cube, crushed*
> *¼ teaspoon salt*
> *¼ teaspoon dried thyme*
> *Pinch of freshly ground black pepper*
> *1 6½-ounce can minced clams with liquid*
> *1 tablespoon chopped fresh parsley leaves*

1. In a large saucepan or Dutch oven, melt the butter over medium heat.
2. Sauté the onion, potato, and celery until tender.
3. Stir the flour into the milk with a wire whisk and pour the mixture into the saucepan. Cook and stir until thickened.
4. Add the bouillon cube, seasonings, and clams with liquid and heat through. Serve immediately garnished with the chopped parsley.

YIELD: 2 generous servings.

Seafood Gumbo

This New Orleans favorite contains a variety of seafood. Vary the ingredients to suit your taste and the market availability. Like most soups, this recipe improves with age, so preparation the day before adds not only to the convenience but to the flavor. Serve it over hot cooked rice.

½ cup all-purpose flour
½ cup vegetable oil
1 cup chopped onion
1 cup chopped celery
1 medium-size sweet green pepper, diced
2 garlic cloves, minced
2 14½-ounce cans chicken broth
1 14½-ounce can Italian plum tomatoes with liquid,
   chopped
½ teaspoon hot red pepper sauce, or to taste
1 teaspoon dried oregano
1 teaspoon dried thyme
Salt to taste
1 pound fresh or frozen crab meat, picked over
1 pound fresh or frozen shrimp, shelled and deveined
1 pint shucked oysters
2 teaspoons gumbo filé powder (see Note)
Chopped fresh parsley leaves

1. In a Dutch oven, combine the flour and oil. Cook over medium heat, stirring constantly, until the mixture is reddish-brown in color. (Flour and oil brown better in a pan without a nonstick finish.)
2. Add the onion, celery, green pepper, and garlic. Sauté until the vegetables are tender, about 5 minutes.
3. Add the chicken broth, tomatoes, hot pepper sauce, and seasonings. Bring to a boil. Lower the heat, cover, and simmer for 1 hour.
4. Add the seafood and simmer, uncovered, for 10 to 15 minutes.
5. Blend 1 tablespoon of the hot liquid into the filé powder; then stir into the gumbo. Adjust the seasonings, if desired.
6. Serve each portion over ½ cup cooked rice in a large soup bowl. Garnish with the chopped parsley.

YIELD: 8 to 10 servings.

NOTE: Gumbo filé can be found in the herb and spice section of your grocery store. It seasons as well as thickens the gumbo.

Swedish Meatballs

These may be served as an appetizer or with noodles as a main dish.

> 1 cup fine dry bread crumbs
> 1/3 cup milk
> 1/4 cup minced onion
> 1 pound lean ground beef
> 1 large egg, beaten
> 1 teaspoon salt
> 1/2 teaspoon ground nutmeg
> Pinch of freshly ground black pepper
> 2 tablespoons butter or margarine
> 2 teaspoons all-purpose flour
> 1 cup hot water
> 1 beef bouillon cube, crumbled
> 1/2 cup milk
> 1/2 cup light cream

1. Combine the bread crumbs and 1/3 cup milk. Add the onion, meat, egg, and seasonings. Shape into 1-inch balls.
2. In a frying pan, melt the butter over medium heat. Sauté the meatballs on all sides until brown. Remove from the pan.
3. Add the flour to the drippings and blend well. Add the water, bouillon cube, 1/2 cup milk, and cream. Cook and stir until thickened.
4. Add the meatballs, cover, and cook over low heat for 10 minutes.

YIELD: 6 servings.

Salisbury Steak

The rich flavor of this recipe delights the diners; the ease of preparation delights the chef! Serve with buttered noodles with parsley and a salad.

1½ *pounds lean ground beef*
⅓ *cup seasoned bread crumbs*
1 *large egg, slightly beaten*
¼ *cup minced onion*
1 *garlic clove, minced*
½ *teaspoon salt*
½ *teaspoon powdered mustard*
Freshly ground black pepper to taste
¼ *cup butter or margarine*
4 *green onions (scallions), sliced*
½ *pound fresh mushrooms, sliced*
3 *tablespoons all-purpose flour*
1 *to* 1½ *cups canned beef broth*

1. Combine the meat, the bread crumbs, egg, onion, garlic, and seasonings. Shape into 6 patties.
2. In a frying pan, melt 1 tablespoon of the butter over medium heat. Brown the patties on both sides. Remove the patties to a plate and set aside.
3. Melt the remaining 3 tablespoons of butter and sauté the green onions and mushrooms lightly.
4. Blend in the flour and pepper to taste. Gradually add the beef broth and stir and cook until thickened.
5. Return the patties to the sauce. Cover and cook over low heat for 15 minutes.

YIELD: 6 servings.

Stuffed Green Peppers

A real classic as far as home cooking is concerned!

4 *medium-size sweet green peppers*
1 *pound lean ground beef*
1 *small onion, chopped*
⅓ *cup quick-cooking rice*
1 *teaspoon dried oregano*
½ *teaspoon salt*
Pinch of freshly ground black pepper
1 8-*ounce can tomato sauce*
¼ *cup Burgundy or other dry red wine*
Grated Parmesan cheese

1. Slice off the stem end of the peppers and remove the seeds.
2. Combine the beef, onion, rice, seasonings, and ¹/₃ cup of the tomato sauce. Stuff the mixture into the peppers.
3. Put the peppers in a saucepan. Pour the remaining tomato sauce and the wine over the peppers.
4. Bring to a boil, cover, and simmer until tender, about 45 minutes. Add a few tablespoons of water if the sauce begins to cook away.
5. Serve with the grated cheese and tomato-wine sauce, if desired.

YIELD: 4 servings.

Meat Loaves with Pesto Sauce

This recipe serves 4 with individual mini-meat loaves. The Pesto Sauce adds an herb and cheese flavor that makes this recipe unique. If you're a family of two, prepare the entire recipe and use the leftovers for sandwiches.

> *1 pound lean ground beef*
> *¹/₂ teaspoon salt*
> *¹/₄ teaspoon freshly ground black pepper*
> *¹/₂ cup seasoned bread crumbs*
> *¹/₄ cup minced onion*
> *3 tablespoons Pesto Sauce (page 168)*
> *1 8-ounce can tomato sauce*
> *1 large egg, beaten*
> *1 tablespoon vegetable oil*
> *¹/₄ cup water*

1. In a mixing bowl, combine the meat, seasonings, bread crumbs, onion, 2 tablespoons of the Pesto Sauce, 2 tablespoons of the tomato sauce, and the egg. Shape into 4 loaves.
2. In a frying pan, heat the oil over medium heat. Brown the meat loaves on all sides.
3. Combine the remaining tomato sauce with the water and the remaining tablespoon of Pesto Sauce. Pour the mixture over the meat. Turn the heat to low, cover, and cook for 20 minutes.
4. Serve the loaves topped with the tomato-pesto sauce.

YIELD: 4 servings.

Eggplant Skillet Dinner

I prepare this quick casserole often when eggplant is in season.

>*1 pound lean ground beef*
>*¼ cup chopped onion*
>*1 tablespoon all-purpose flour*
>*1 8-ounce can tomato sauce*
>*¾ cup water*
>*¼ cup chopped sweet green pepper*
>*1 teaspoon chili powder*
>*1 small eggplant, cut into ½-inch slices*
>*½ teaspoon salt*
>*1 cup shredded sharp processed American cheese*
>*Grated Parmesan cheese*

1. In a frying pan, brown the beef and onion over medium heat. Drain off any excess fat.
2. Stir in the flour, tomato sauce, water, green pepper, and chili powder.
3. Top with the eggplant slices and sprinkle with the salt. Cover and simmer until the eggplant is tender, about 15 minutes.
4. Top the eggplant with the cheese. Cover and cook until the cheese melts. Serve sprinkled with grated cheese.

YIELD: 4 servings.

One-Hour Spaghetti Sauce

This basic recipe can be adapted to your personal taste through the simple addition of herbs and spices. Be creative if you like! My version uses the secret ingredient, cinnamon, to add extra spark. What will yours be? Serve the sauce over cooked thin spaghetti.

>*1 pound lean ground beef*
>*1 medium-size onion, chopped*
>*1 garlic clove, minced*
>*1 28-ounce can tomato sauce*
>*1 6-ounce can tomato paste*
>*1 cup water*
>*1 4-ounce can sliced mushrooms, drained (continued)*

 1 teaspoon salt
 ½ teaspoon dried basil
 ½ teaspoon dried oregano
 Pinch of ground cinnamon

1. In a frying pan, brown the meat, onion, and garlic over medium heat. Drain off any excess fat.
2. Stir in tomato sauce, tomato paste, water, mushrooms, and seasonings. Cover and simmer over low heat for 45 minutes.

YIELD: 4 servings.

NOTE: This recipe improves with age, so you may want to prepare it ahead for added flavor and convenience.

Lots o' Chili

Chili should be prepared in quantity because it cooks better in volume. Chili freezes well and can be packaged in serving-size portions to be eaten weeks or even months later. Serve this chili with No-Oven Bacon Corn Bread (page 174) or French bread.

 2 pounds lean ground beef
 4 medium-size onions, chopped
 1 sweet green pepper, diced
 2 garlic cloves, minced
 3 to 5 tablespoons chili powder, or to taste
 2 teaspoons salt
 1 29-ounce can tomato purée
 1 cup water
 1 30-ounce can red kidney beans, drained
 2 teaspoons ground cumin

1. In a Dutch oven, brown the meat, onions, and green pepper over medium heat. Drain off any excess fat.
2. Add the garlic, seasonings, tomato purée, and water. Cover and simmer for 1 hour.
3. Add the beans and cumin. Cover and simmer for 15 minutes. Serve in large soup bowls.

YIELD: 8 servings.

NOTE: This recipe may be doubled, if desired.

Texas No-Bean Chili

This hearty recipe is a bit different from the traditional because it uses chopped meat instead of ground beef and adds cornmeal to thicken the stew. Try this one when the cold winter winds blow.

> 2 to 3 tablespoons butter or margarine
> 2 pounds round steak, cut into ½-inch cubes
> 2 large onions, chopped
> 2 garlic cloves, minced
> 2 14½-ounce cans whole tomatoes with liquid, chopped
> 1 cup water
> ¾ cup dry red wine
> 1 to 2 tablespoons chili powder
> 2 teaspoons ground cumin
> 2 teaspoons dried oregano
> 1 teaspoon dried basil
> Salt to taste
> ¼ cup cornmeal
> 2 tablespoons chopped fresh parsley leaves

1. In a Dutch oven, melt the butter over medium heat. Brown the meat on all sides. Add the onions and garlic and cook until the onions are soft.
2. Add the tomatoes, water, ½ cup of the wine, and seasonings. Cover and simmer until the meat is tender, about 1½ hours.
3. Combine the remaining wine and cornmeal and stir into the meat mixture. Cook until thickened. Sprinkle with parsley and serve.

YIELD: 8 servings.

NOTE: This recipe freezes well.

Green Chile Stew

This is a favorite regional dish of the Southwest. I first experienced this well-seasoned hearty meal while visiting a friend in New Mexico. She served this stew with a guacamole salad and passed hot flour tortillas. Don't be afraid of the chiles, they are very mild.

> *2 pounds round steak, cut into 1½-inch cubes*
> *¼ cup all-purpose flour*
> *Salt and freshly ground black pepper*
> *2 tablespoons vegetable oil*
> *2 large onions, chopped*
> *2 4-ounce cans chopped green chiles, drained*
> *1 14½-ounce can whole tomatoes with liquid, chopped*
> *1 cup water*
> *1 garlic clove, minced*

1. Dredge the meat in the flour seasoned with a pinch of salt and pepper.
2. In a Dutch oven, heat the oil. Brown the meat on all sides. Add onions and cook until the onions are soft.
3. Add all the remaining ingredients. Season with about 1 teaspoon of salt. Cover and simmer until the meat is tender, about 1 hour.

YIELD: 6 servings.

Hungarian Goulash

You can't beat the flavor of this ethnic dish, but unlike many stews, this one is simple to prepare and ready to eat in 1 hour. Use real Hungarian paprika if you like spicy food. Serve the goulash with hot cooked noodles and a tossed green salad.

> *1 pound boneless round steak, cut into 1-inch cubes*
> *1 pound lean veal, cut into 1-inch cubes*
> *All-purpose flour*
> *1 tablespoon vegetable oil*
> *1 large onion, chopped*
> *2 garlic cloves, minced*
> *1 tablespoon paprika*
> *1 teaspoon dried thyme*
> *Salt and freshly ground black pepper to taste*
> *1½ cups canned beef broth*
> *2 tablespoons tomato paste*
> *Sour cream, optional*

1. Dredge the meat in the flour.
2. In a Dutch oven, heat the oil over medium heat. Brown the meat on all sides. Add the onion, garlic, and seasonings. Sauté until the onion is soft.

3. Add the beef broth and tomato paste. Cover and simmer until the meat is tender, about 1 hour. Add additional broth if necessary.
4. Stir a dollop or two of sour cream into the sauce, if desired.

YIELD: 8 servings.

Flemish Beef Stew

I dined on this delightful rich, thick stew in a small French country restaurant while traveling in Brussels. The dark beer and mustard adds a special touch to this classic dish. Serve it with a mixed green salad, rye bread, and a glass of cold dark beer.

3 pounds boneless beef chuck roast, cut into 1½-inch cubes
¼ cup all-purpose flour
1 tablespoon dried thyme
½ teaspoon salt
¼ teaspoon freshly ground black pepper
6 slices bacon
2 large onions, chopped
2 cups dark beer
2 tablespoons Dijon mustard
2 teaspoons sugar
1 tablespoon fresh lemon juice
Chopped fresh parsley leaves

1. Dredge the beef in a mixture of the flour, thyme, salt, and pepper.
2. In a Dutch oven, fry the bacon over medium-high heat until crisp. Remove the bacon and drain on paper towels.
3. Brown half of the beef on all sides in the bacon drippings. Remove the browned beef to a plate and repeat with the remaining beef. Remove all the beef from the pan.
4. Sauté the onions until soft. Return the beef to the pan and add all the remaining ingredients except the reserved bacon and the parsley. Bring to a boil, lower the heat, cover, and simmer for 2 hours, or until the meat is tender.
5. Serve in large soup bowls. Sprinkle each serving with crumbled bacon and chopped parsley.

YIELD: 6 to 8 servings.

American Beef Stew

This is a country-style recipe that brings back memories of warm family gatherings and delicious aromas. Serve this stew over cooked noodles or with Parsley Drop Dumplings (page 172) to complete this one-pot meal.

> *2 pounds boneless beef stew meat, cut into 1½-inch cubes*
> *All-purpose flour*
> *2 tablespoons butter or margarine*
> *2 tablespoons vegetable oil*
> *1 teaspoon salt*
> *¼ teaspoon freshly ground black pepper*
> *1 bay leaf*
> *½ teaspoon dried thyme*
> *1 cup beer (or canned beef broth)*
> *1 cup water*
> *1 large onion, cut into chunks*
> *2 celery stalks, sliced into 1-inch pieces*
> *4 medium-size potatoes, quartered*
> *6 carrots, peeled and cut into diagonal 1-inch slices*
> *1 10-ounce package frozen peas*
> *½ cup water or beer*

1. Dredge the meat in the flour.
2. In a Dutch oven, heat the butter and oil over medium-high heat. Brown half of the beef on all sides. Remove the browned beef to a plate and brown the remaining meat. Add more fat if necessary. Return all the beef to the pan.
3. Add the seasonings, beer, and water to the pan. Cover and simmer for 1½ hours.
4. Add all vegetables except the peas. Continue to cook for 30 minutes, or until the vegetables and meat are tender.
5. Remove the bay leaf and stir in the peas. Combine 2 tablespoons of flour with the ½ cup of water or beer. Stir the flour mixture into the meat. Cook until thickened.

YIELD: 8 servings.

Quick Sauerbraten

This dish has all the flavor of traditional recipes that take three or more days to marinate. Serve with hot cooked noodles.

½ cup water
½ cup white vinegar
2 teaspoons sugar
½ teaspoon salt
4 whole black peppercorns
Pinch of ground ginger
1 small onion, sliced
1 bay leaf
4 whole cloves
1 pound beef top round steak, cut into 2- by ½-inch strips
¼ cup crushed gingersnap cookies
2 tablespoons vegetable oil
2 carrots, peeled and sliced thin
2 celery stalks, cut thin on the diagonal

1. Combine the water, vinegar, sugar, salt, peppercorns, and ginger in a large mixing bowl.
2. Stir in the onion, bay leaf, and cloves. Ad the beef and stir well to coat the meat with the marinade. Cover and refrigerate 30 minutes.
3. Discard the bay leaf, cloves, and peppercorns from the marinade. Drain the marinade into a bowl; then stir the gingersnaps into the marinade. Set it aside.
4. Preheat a wok or skillet over high heat. Add the oil. Sauté the carrots and celery until tender. Remove to a plate.
5. Add half of the meat and onions. Sauté until done, about 3 minutes. Remove and repeat with the remaining meat and onions. Return all the meat to the pan.
6. Push the meat to the sides of the pan and add the marinade mixture. Cook and stir until thickened. Return the vegetables to the pan and stir all the ingredients together. Heat through. Serve immediately.

YIELD: 4 servings.

Old-Fashioned Hash

This is a tasty way to use leftover beef. Serve it for dinner with a salad or for brunch topped with poached eggs.

> *2 tablespoons butter or margarine*
> *1 medium-size onion, chopped*
> *2 cups diced peeled potatoes*
> *2 cups cooked ½-inch beef cubes*
> *Pinch of garlic salt*
> *Salt and freshly ground black pepper to taste*
> *Chopped fresh parsley leaves*

1. In a frying pan, melt the butter over medium heat. Sauté the onion and potatoes until soft.
2. Add the beef and seasonings and cook until heated through. Garnish each serving with chopped parsley.

YIELD: 4 servings.

Swiss Steak

The tomatoes not only add a wonderful flavor and color to this dish, but they also tenderize the meat as it cooks. Serve with cooked noodles or mashed potatoes.

> *¼ cup all-purpose flour*
> *1 teaspoon salt*
> *¼ teaspoon freshly ground black pepper*
> *2 pounds round steak, cut 1 inch thick*
> *2 tablespoons vegetable oil*
> *1 large onion, sliced*
> *1 14½-ounce can whole tomatoes with liquid, chopped*

1. Combine the flour, salt, and pepper. Using a meat tenderizing mallet, pound the flour mixture into the meat.
2. In a frying pan, heat the oil over medium-high heat. Brown the meat on both sides.
3. Lay the onion slices and tomatoes over the meat. Cover and simmer for 1½ hours, or until the meat is tender.

YIELD: 6 servings.

Creamed Dried Beef

This is an old-fashioned recipe that is a great lifesaver when time is short. It's also a favorite with hearty eaters.

2 tablespoons butter or margarine
2 tablespoons all-purpose flour
1 cup milk
Pinch of freshly ground black pepper
Dash of hot pepper sauce
1 8-ounce can peas, drained
4 ounces dried beef, cut into 1-inch pieces
Toast points

1. In a frying pan or saucepan, melt the butter over medium heat. Then blend in the flour to form a paste. Slowly add the milk and cook and stir until thick.
2. Add the pepper, hot pepper sauce, peas, and beef and heat through. Serve on toast points.

YIELD: 2 servings.

Ratatouille and Sausage Casserole

This great summer dish abounds with fresh garden vegetables, yet it's hearty enough to satisfy any large appetite. Serve with a garden salad and French bread.

1 medium-size eggplant, peeled and cut into 1-inch squares
Salt
4 to 6 sweet or hot Italian sausage links
4 medium-size zucchini, trimmed and sliced
2 medium-size sweet green peppers, cut into 1-inch pieces
2 large ripe tomatoes, diced
1 medium-size onion, chopped
2 garlic cloves, minced
1 15-ounce can tomato sauce with herbs
1 teaspoon dried basil
1 teaspoon dried oregano

1. Sprinkle the cut eggplant lightly with salt. Let stand for 5 minutes. Drain.

2. In a frying pan, brown the sausages over low heat. Drain off any excess fat.
3. Add the remaining ingredients, cover, and simmer until the vegetables are tender, about 40 minutes.

YIELD: 4 servings.

NOTE: This recipe freezes well.

Spareribs and Sauerkraut

This one-pot meal is easy to fix and reheats perfectly if advance preparation is necessary. Serve with parslied boiled potatoes.

> *2 tablespoons vegetable oil*
> *3 pounds pork spareribs*
> *Salt and freshly ground black pepper to taste*
> *1 1-pound, 11-ounce can sauerkraut with liquid*
> *1 large apple, chopped*
> *2 tablespoons brown sugar*
> *1 tablespoon caraway seeds*

1. In a Dutch oven, heat the oil over medium-high heat. Brown the meat on all sides.
2. Add all the remaining ingredients to the pan, cover and simmer for 1½ hours. Skim off any excess fat before serving.

YIELD: 6 servings.

Lamb Stew

Lamb lovers find this herbed recipe a real treat. Serve it with cooked noodles or Parsley Drop Dumplings (page 172) and a mixed green salad.

> *3 tablespoons vegetable oil*
> *¼ cup all-purpose flour*
> *Salt and freshly ground black pepper to taste*
> *1½ pounds boneless lamb, cut into 1-inch cubes*
> *2 garlic cloves, minced*

3 cups water
½ teaspoon dried oregano
½ teaspoon dried basil
4 carrots, peeled and cut into 1-inch chunks
3 potatoes, peeled and cut into 1-inch cubes
1 medium-size onion, cubed
1 10-ounce package frozen peas
Chopped fresh parsley leaves

1. In a Dutch oven, heat the oil over medium-high heat.
2. Put the flour and salt and pepper in a small paper bag. Add a few pieces of meat at a time to the bag. Shake to coat evenly. Repeat until all the meat is coated.
3. Brown the meat on all sides in the oil.
4. Add the garlic and water to the pan. Cover and simmer for 1 hour.
5. Add the seasonings and vegetables except the peas and parsley to the pan. Cook, uncovered, for 20 minutes.
6. Add the peas and parsley and heat through.

YIELD: 6 servings.

Liver Sauté with Bacon and Herbs

For liver connoisseurs, this herbed recipe is superb.

4 slices bacon, cut into ½-inch pieces
1 medium-size onion, sliced
1 pound sliced calf's or baby beef liver
All-purpose flour
¼ cup dry sherry
¼ cup water
½ teaspoon dried rosemary, crushed
½ teaspoon dried basil
Salt and freshly ground black pepper to taste

1. In a frying pan, sauté the bacon over medium heat until crisp. Remove the bacon and drain it on paper towels. Sauté the onion in the bacon drippings until it is soft. Remove the onion to a plate.
2. Dredge the liver in the flour and sauté it for 2 minutes on

each side. Add the sherry, water, and herbs. Season with salt and pepper and simmer for 5 minutes. Return the onion and bacon to the pan and heat through.

YIELD: 4 servings.

Potato Pancakes

This recipe stands on its own. Serve the pancakes with spiced applesauce and a dollop of sour cream.

> *6 medium-size potatoes, peeled*
> *2 large eggs, beaten*
> *2 tablespoons all-purpose flour*
> *2 teaspoons grated onion*
> *1 teaspoon salt*
> *Pinch of freshly ground black pepper*
> *Vegetable oil*

1. Using the large holes of a grater, shred the potatoes into cold water to avoid their darkening. Drain off any excess liquid and pat the potatoes dry with paper towels.
2. Combine all the ingredients except the oil in a bowl.
3. Add enough oil to a skillet to make a ½-inch depth. Heat the oil to 375 degrees over medium-high heat.
4. For each pancake, drop ¼ cup of the batter into the oil. Flatten with a spatula and cook until golden; turn and cook on the other side. Remove the pancakes to paper towels to drain. Repeat until all the pancakes are cooked.

YIELD: 4 servings.

Peasant Beans and Pasta

This is a typical peasant country dish that is long on flavor, hearty, and easy to prepare. Serve with crisp French bread and a full-bodied red wine.

½ *pound elbow or shell macaroni*
3 *tablespoons olive oil*
½ *pound dried Great Northern*
 beans, or 1 16-ounce can white
 beans
6 *slices bacon, cut into* ½-*inch pieces*
1 *large onion, chopped*
2 *carrots, peeled and diced*
⅓ *cup minced fresh parsley leaves*
2 *tablespoons dried basil*
1 *tablespoon dried oregano*
1 14½-*ounce can whole tomatoes*
 with liquid, chopped
¼ *cup dry red wine*
Salt and freshly ground black pepper
 to taste
2 *tablespoons butter or margarine*
⅓ *cup grated Parmesan cheese*
Chopped fresh parsley leaves for
 garnish

1. In a Dutch oven, cook the pasta in boiling salted water until *al dente*. Drain and toss with 1 tablespoon of the olive oil. Set aside.
2. Sort and wash the dried beans. Put them into the Dutch oven and cover them with cold water. Cover the pan and bring the water to a boil; boil for 3 minutes. Remove the pan from the heat and let the beans stand for 1 hour.
3. Return the beans to the heat and cook them over low heat until they are tender, about 30 minutes. Drain the beans and reserve ¼ cup of the cooking liquid. (If using canned beans, drain them and reserve ¼ cup of the liquid.)
4. In the Dutch oven, heat remaining 2 tablespoons of olive oil over medium heat. Sauté the bacon until partially cooked. Add onion, carrots, and herbs. Sauté until the vegetables are soft.
5. Add the tomatoes, bean liquid, wine, and salt and pepper. Cover and simmer for 10 minutes.
6. Add the cooked beans, cover, and simmer for 20 minutes.
7. Add the pasta, butter, and cheese and heat through. Serve in large soup bowls garnished with the chopped parsley.

YIELD: 8 servings.

Macaroni and Two-Cheese Casserole

This no-bake version of the old favorite uses unconventional ingredients for a savory taste.

> *2 cups elbow macaroni*
> *2 tablespoons olive oil*
> *6 green onions (scallions), sliced*
> *1 garlic clove, minced*
> *1 sweet green pepper, sliced thin*
> *½ teaspoon salt*
> *½ teaspoon freshly ground black pepper*
> *½ teaspoon dried basil*
> *1 15-ounce container ricotta cheese*
> *1 cup shredded Cheddar cheese*
> *½ cup milk*
> *1 large egg, beaten*
> *Chopped fresh parsley leaves*

1. In a large saucepan, cook the macaroni according to package directions. Drain and set aside.
2. In the same saucepan, heat the oil over medium heat. Sauté the onions, garlic, and green pepper until tender. Add the seasonings and quickly stir in all the remaining ingredients. Add the macaroni and toss well to coat. Heat until warmed through. Spoon into a serving bowl and serve immediately.

YIELD: 4 to 6 servings.

SUGGESTED
COUNTRY COOKING MENUS

· *FALL SUNDAY EVENING SUPPER*

American Beef Stew (page 112)
with
Parsley Drop Dumplings (page 172)
Mixed Green Salad
Caramel-Peach Upside-Down Cake (page 196)
Beverage

· *AFTER SKI GATHERING* ·
Hot Spiced Wine
Hearty Vegetable Soup (page 97)
Beer and Cheese Rarebit (page 47)
Chocolate Fondue (page 189)
Beverage

· *FRIDAY SUPPER SPECIAL* ·
Applesauce
Potato Pancakes (page 118)
Sour Cream
Peach Melba Sundae (page 195)
Beverage

· *MIDWEEK FEAST* ·
Salisbury Steak (page 104)
Cooked Noodles
Tossed Salad
Autumn Baked Apples (page 183)
Beverage

· *NO TIME TO COOK* ·
Lots o' Chili (page 108)
(Prepared ahead)
French Bread
Fresh Fruit Compote (page 187)
Beverage

· *LAZY SUMMER EVENING* ·
Eggplant Skillet Dinner (page 107)
Garden Salad
Marinated Melon (page 188)
Iced Tea

7
Company's Coming

If company is coming and you have a small kitchen, are short on time, or feel your culinary skills need polish, *relax*! Help is on the pages of this chapter. This book is all about simple meals cooked on *one burner*, in one pot or pan. This approach will also save your dinner party and let you enjoy your company whether you've invited the "boss," a date, or relatives.

Cooking styles have changed today, making it easier than ever to entertain in a simple, but elegant, manner. It is no longer necessary to cook all day when you've invited guests. Pasta dishes and sautéed meat or fish with a light sauce are good choices. If desired, an appetizer can be served as a first course. Add a pretty salad, a basket of bread, an excellent bottle of wine, and a memorable dessert to complete the meal. And don't forget the finishing touches—soft music and fresh flowers.

How to Give a Great Party!

"The more you do ahead for your party, the better the party." This has been proven time and again. The following tips will help you to dazzle your guests and allow you to have fun at your own party.

· Plan the menu at least a week ahead. This will give you a chance to shop for all the ingredients, especially any hard-to-find ones. It will also allow you to shop the food specials during the week.

· When planning the menu, always keep it simple. A well-prepared entrée, a salad, a vegetable, and a glamorous dessert are all that are needed to entertain even the best of friends or relatives.

· The day before the party, schedule the meal preparation. Decide what can be prepared ahead and what must be delayed for the final moment. Making a written time schedule can be a real help.

· If you're serving wine, purchase it ahead and chill it, if necessary.

· Plan an appetizer if you want time to linger before the meal is served. Again, keep it simple, light, and make sure it complements the entrée.

· Buy fresh flowers the day before so they're at the height of their bloom for the party.

· Set the table before your guests arrive. If possible, plan to have a seasonal theme to the table for real fun.

· If you're preparing a last-minute entrée, such as Fettuccine Alfredo, invite the guests to join you in the kitchen if there's room, and if you've been tidy throughout the preparation!

· Consider guest participation if your kitchen allows. Let guests prepare an Oriental recipe or two from chapter 8 (page 142) for a relaxed gathering.

· If you have a small table, you might want to consider fixing the plates for each guest in the kitchen. It saves space and allows you to garnish to your heart's content.

· Clear the table before dessert is served. Serve the coffee and unveil the dessert. If you entertain often, consider the purhase of a coffee maker that has a portable serving carafe that will keep the coffee warm at the table.

· Plan a dessert that is the perfect ending to your great meal. Consider the type of meal you're serving before selecting a recipe. A heavy entrée begs for a light, refreshing finale; a light meal allows you to splurge on dessert!

· If desired, cordials can be served either at the table or in the living room.

· As the host or hostess, be sure to schedule a few moments before your guests arrive for a quiet time just for you!

· Relax and enjoy!

Steak Diane

This gourmet recipe is recommended for that extra-special evening for two! Serve it with a side dish of pasta and a green salad. A good red wine is also a must!

> *2 6-ounce beef tenderloin fillets*
> *1 tablespoon all-purpose flour*
> *¼ teaspoon salt*
> *Pinch of freshly ground black pepper*
> *¼ cup butter or margarine*
> *1 tablespoon Dijon mustard*
> *6 ounces fresh mushrooms, sliced*
> *2 green onions (scallions), sliced*
> *2 teaspoons Worcestershire sauce*
> *¼ cup Cognac*
> *½ cup canned beef broth*
> *Chopped fresh parsley leaves, optional*

1. Pound the steak with a meat mallet or the back of a large knife. Coat the meat with a mixture of flour, salt, and pepper.
2. In a frying pan, melt 1 tablespoon of the butter over medium-high heat. Brown the meat quickly, 1 minute on each side. Remove the meat to a platter. Spread the meat with mustard on both sides; then set it aside.
3. Melt the remaining butter in the same pan. Sauté the mushrooms and onions over medium heat until soft.
4. Add the Worcestershire sauce; then add the Cognac and ignite it with a long match. Let the flames burn out and then add the beef broth.
5. Return the steaks to the frying pan and cook to the desired doneness, turning once. Serve garnished with chopped fresh parsley, if desired.

YIELD: 2 servings.

Tenderloins with Vermouth

When you want to serve a spectacular meal, consider this easy recipe. Serve it with pasta and a salad of mixed greens with a creamy herbed dressing and crisp dinner rolls.

1 tablespoon vegetable oil
1 garlic clove
4 beef tenderloin fillets, cut 1 inch thick
1 pound fresh mushrooms, sliced
6 green onions (scallions), sliced
¼ cup dry vermouth
1 13-ounce can mushroom gravy
Salt and freshly ground black pepper to taste

1. In a frying pan, heat the oil over medium heat. Sauté the garlic until it is brown. Remove and discard the garlic.
2. Sauté the fillets on both sides until browned. Remove to a platter.
3. Sauté the mushrooms and onions until soft.
4. Add the vermouth and gravy to the pan and season with salt and pepper. Return the fillets to the pan, cover the pan, and cook over low heat for 5 minutes for medium (for rare, just heat the fillet through in the sauce).

YIELD: 4 servings.

Ham Steak Aloha

The sweet-and-sour flavor of the sauce is perfect with a ham slice. If you need a quick meal for guests on a work night, this is definitely one to consider.

½ cup packed brown sugar
¼ cup butter or margarine
¼ cup dry white wine or reserved pineapple juice
1 1½-pound ham steak
1 16-ounce can pineapple chunks, drained and liquid reserved

1. In a skillet, combine the sugar, butter, and wine. Heat over medium heat until smooth. Add the ham and cook for 5 minutes on each side.
2. Remove the ham to a platter and keep it warm. Add the pineapple chunks to the pan and cook for 5 minutes. Spoon the pineapple sauce over the ham and serve immediately.

YIELD: 4 to 6 servings.

Veal Piccata

This is a classic dish that requires little preparation time and little cooking time. It's just the ticket on those busy days.

12 veal scallops (thin slices of leg of veal), 1½ pounds total weight
½ cup all-purpose flour
⅓ cup butter or margarine
⅓ cup dry white wine
3 tablespoons fresh lemon juice
Salt and freshly ground black pepper to taste
1 tablespoon chopped fresh parsley leaves

1. Dredge the veal in the flour.
2. In a frying pan, melt the butter over medium heat. Sauté the veal until lightly brown on both sides.
3. Add the wine and lemon juice to the pan and season the veal with salt and pepper. Cover and simmer until the veal is tender, about 5 minutes.
4. Remove the veal to a serving platter and pour the sauce over it. Sprinkle with parsley and serve at once.

YIELD: 4 servings.

Chicken Cacciatore

This Italian dish looks and tastes as though you've spent hours in the kitchen, but would you believe 45 minutes? Serve with pasta, crusty Italian or French bread, and a crisp salad.

¼ cup all-purpose flour
1½ teaspoons salt
1 teaspoon paprika
Pinch of freshly ground black pepper
1 3-pound chicken, cut into serving pieces
¼ cup vegetable or olive oil
1 medium-size onion, minced
1 8-ounce can mushroom slices, drained
1 14½-ounce can whole tomatoes with liquid, chopped
1 6-ounce can tomato paste
1 garlic clove, minced
Hot pepper sauce to taste
¾ cup dry red wine

1. Put the flour, salt, paprika, and pepper in a plastic bag. Shake several chicken parts in the mixture at a time to coat them thoroughly. Set aside.
2. In a skillet, heat the oil over medium heat. Brown the chicken parts on all sides. Add the onion and mushrooms. Cook until the onion is lightly browned.
3. Add the tomatoes, tomato paste, garlic, and hot pepper sauce. Cover and simmer over low heat until the chicken is tender, about 30 minutes. Add the wine and heat through.

YIELD: 4 servings.

Chicken in Green Peppercorn Sauce

This is an elegant dish that is served in many fine restaurants. The green peppercorns add a mild well-seasoned flavor. The dish goes very well with pasta and a nice green salad.

> *2 tablespoons butter or margarine*
> *2 whole chicken breasts, skinned, boned, and halved*
> *2 green onions (scallions), sliced*
> *1 tablespoon all-purpose flour*
> *½ cup light cream*
> *¼ cup canned chicken broth*
> *1 teaspoon drained green peppercorns (see Note)*
> *¼ teaspoon salt*
> *¼ cup dry white wine*

1. In a skillet, melt the butter over medium heat. Sauté the chicken breast halves for 5 minutes on each side. Remove to a platter.
2. Sauté the onions until they are soft. Stir in the flour. Then quickly stir in the cream, chicken broth, peppercorns, and salt. Cook and stir until the sauce has thickened.
3. Stir in the wine and return the chicken to the pan. Heat through.

YIELD: 4 servings.

NOTE: Green peppercorns are available in the gourmet food sections of grocery stores.

Mustard-Herb Chicken Breasts

If company is coming and you don't have time to fuss, here's a recipe to keep in mind. Serve with a purchased salad, dinner rolls, and Fresh Fruit Compote (page 187).

¼ cup Dijon mustard
½ teaspoon dried thyme
¼ teaspoon salt
Pinch of freshly ground black pepper
2 whole chicken breasts, skinned, boned, and halved
½ cup dry bread crumbs
2 to 3 tablespoons butter or margarine
1 tablespoon fresh lemon juice

1. Combine the mustard, thyme, salt, and pepper in a small bowl. Spread the mustard mixture on both sides of the chicken. Then coat the chicken with the bread crumbs.
2. In a frying pan, melt the butter over medium heat. Sauté the chicken on both sides until brown and cooked through, about 3 to 5 minutes on each side.
3. Just before serving, sprinkle with the lemon juice.

YIELD: 4 servings.

NOTE: This breaded chicken breast is also delicious when served on a hard roll with a sliced-tomato-and-lettuce garnish.

Chicken with Green Grapes

Grapes add an unusual sweet tang to the chicken breasts and serve as an attractive garnish. Serve the dish with hot cooked rice.

2 tablespoons butter or margarine
2 whole chicken breasts, skinned, boned, and cut into 1-inch pieces
1 cup sliced fresh mushrooms
2 green onions (scallions), sliced
2 teaspoons cornstarch
⅓ cup canned chicken broth
1 cup halved seedless green grapes
¼ cup dry white wine

1. In a skillet or wok, melt the butter over medium heat. Sauté the chicken pieces, mushrooms, and onions until the chicken is done, about 5 minutes.
2. Combine the cornstarch and broth and add to the skillet. Cook and stir until thickened. Add the grapes and wine and heat through. Serve immediately.

YIELD: 4 servings.

Chicken in a Packet

This is a unique way to cook individual servings of chicken. It not only keeps them moist, but it also saves on cleanup! Serve with a vegetable salad.

> *2 whole chicken breasts, skinned, boned, and halved*
> *2 green onions (scallions), sliced*
> *1 tablespoon chopped fresh parsley leaves*
> *½ cup fresh lemon juice*
> *Pinch of garlic salt*
> *Pinch of lemon pepper*
> *¼ cup butter or margarine*

1. Place each piece of chicken on a separate sheet of aluminum foil. Sprinkle each breast with onions, parsley, lemon juice, garlic salt, and lemon pepper. Top with a pat of butter.
2. Seal each packet tightly. Place on a rack in a skillet or Dutch oven. Add enough water to reach the top of the rack. Cover and steam for 20 minutes.

YIELD: 4 servings.

NOTE: This recipe can also be used with fish fillets and shelled shrimp.

Chicken-Artichoke Royal

If you like artichokes and mushrooms you'll love this gourmet recipe sparked with a touch of white wine. It is delicious when served with rice.

2 whole chicken breasts, skinned, boned, and halved
All-purpose flour
¼ cup butter or margarine
¼ pound mushrooms, sliced
1 15-ounce can artichoke hearts, rinsed and well drained
½ cup canned chicken broth
¼ cup dry white wine
2 tablespoons fresh lemon juice
Salt and freshly ground black pepper to taste

1. Coat the chicken with flour on all sides.
2. In a skillet, melt the butter over medium heat. Sauté the chicken until it is golden brown and cooked through. Remove to a platter and cover with aluminum foil to keep it warm.
3. Add the mushrooms to the hot skillet and sauté for 2 minutes. Stir in the artichokes, broth, wine, lemon juice, and seasonings. Cook, stirring occasionally, until the liquid is reduced slightly. Return the chicken to the skillet and heat through. Serve immediately.

YIELD: 4 servings.

Creamy Chicken and Vegetable Suprême

The color of the vegetables and the succulent gravy make this a memorable meal for your guests.

2 tablespoons butter or margarine
1 pound skinned and boned chicken breasts, cut into strips
3 cups canned chicken broth
1 8-ounce package egg noodles
2 green onions (scallions), sliced
2 medium-size zucchini, sliced
1 mild sweet red pepper, diced
1 cup sliced fresh mushrooms
1 cup bottled buttermilk salad dressing
Chopped fresh parsley leaves

1. In a skillet or Dutch oven, melt the butter over medium heat. Brown the chicken on all sides.

2. Add the chicken broth and bring to a boil. Stir in the noodles and vegetables, cover, and simmer, stirring occasionally, for 10 minutes, or until the noodles are tender.
3. Stir in the dressing and heat through. Garnish with the parsley and serve in a pretty casserole.

YIELD: 4 servings.

Sautéed Chicken Livers with Raspberries

Looking for the unusual? This is an easy recipe that is perfect for a special dinner or even a late morning brunch. Serve the chicken livers over wild rice with a crisp green salad on the side.

> 1/4 cup butter or margarine
> 6 green onions (scallions), sliced
> 3/4 cup all-purpose flour
> 1/2 teaspoon salt
> 1/4 teaspoon freshly ground black pepper
> Pinch of ground nutmeg
> 1 pound fresh chicken livers, washed and well dried
> 1/4 cup raspberry vinegar
> 1/3 cup heavy cream
> 3/4 cup fresh raspberries

1. In a skillet, melt the butter over medium heat. Sauté the onions. Then set the pan aside.
2. In a plastic bag, combine the flour and dry seasonings. Shake the livers in the flour mixture a few at a time. Shake off any excess flour.
3. Return the skillet to the heat. When hot, sauté the livers until lightly browned. Remove to a platter and keep warm.
4. Add the vinegar to the skillet. Stir and cook until thickened.
5. Quickly stir in the cream and cook until smooth and thick.
6. Stir in the raspberries and heat through briefly. Arrange the liver on plates, top with the sauce, and serve immediately.

YIELD: 2 servings.

NOTE: Double the recipe, if desired.

Vegetable and Fish Sauté

This very colorful recipe is ready in less than 15 minutes, perfect for an after-work dinner party. I like to use orange roughy, which is a sweet, tender fish that sautés well. Except for the potatoes, I always use fresh ingredients and add lemon pepper for that "special" touch.

2 tablespoons butter or margarine
1 16-ounce can whole new potatoes, drained
1 carrot, peeled and cut into matchsticks
1 medium-size zucchini, trimmed and cut into matchsticks
2 green onions (scallions), sliced
½ cup sliced fresh mushrooms
¾ pound fresh orange roughy or sole fillets
1 tablespoon all-purpose flour
Salt to taste
Pinch of lemon pepper
1 tablespoon fresh lemon juice
Chopped fresh parsley leaves
Fresh ripe tomato slices

1. In a frying pan, melt the butter over medium heat. Sauté the vegetables until they are crisp-tender, about 3 to 4 minutes. Remove to a platter.
2. Dredge the fish in the flour. Sauté the fish on one side until lightly browned. Turn the fish over carefully. Add another tablespoon of butter, if necessary.
3. Top the fish with the vegetables. Season with salt and pepper and sprinkle with lemon juice.
4. Cook, covered, until the fish flakes easily when tested with a fork, about 3 minutes.
5. Arrange the fish fillets on plates. Top with the matchstick vegetables and place the potatoes to the side. Garnish the plates with the chopped parsley and sliced tomatoes.

YIELD: 2 servings.

Perch Amandine

For fish lovers, this is a classic recipe. Serve it with a salad.

2 pounds ocean perch fillets
Fresh lemon juice
All-purpose flour
⅓ cup butter or margarine
1 15-ounce can whole potatoes, drained, or 8 to 12
    small new potatoes, cooked and jackets removed
⅔ cup slivered blanched almonds
Salt and freshly ground black pepper to taste
Chopped fresh parsley leaves

1. Dip the fillets in lemon juice; then dust them with flour.
2. In a skillet, melt the butter over medium heat. Sauté the
   fillets and potatoes until lightly browned on both sides. Remove the fish and potatoes to a serving platter and keep
   warm.
3. Add the almonds to the skillet. Brown them lightly. Season
   with salt and pepper.
4. Add 2 tablespoons of lemon juice to the skillet and pour the
   almonds and sauce over the fillets.
5. Garnish the potatoes with chopped parsley and serve immediately.

YIELD: 4 to 6 servings.

Gazpacho-Sauced Cod

Pretty, low calorie, and quick aptly describe this company dish.

2 tablespoons vegetable oil
1 medium-size onion, chopped
1 medium-size sweet green pepper, diced
1½ cups canned tomato juice
2 medium-size ripe tomatoes, peeled, seeded, and diced
1 pound frozen cod fillets, thawed
½ cup peeled and diced cucumber
Dash of hot red pepper sauce
Salt and freshly ground black pepper to taste
1 tablespoon minced fresh parsley leaves

1. In a frying pan, heat the oil over medium heat. Sauté the
   onion and green pepper until tender.

2. Add the tomato juice and tomatoes and top with the fish fillets. Sprinkle with the cucumber and seasonings.
3. Simmer over low heat until the fish flakes easily when tested with a fork, about 10 to 15 minutes. Garnish with the minced parsley and serve immediately.

YIELD: 4 servings.

Simple Scampi

This recipe will dazzle any shrimp lover.

> *½ cup butter or margarine*
> *¼ cup minced onion*
> *3 garlic cloves, minced*
> *1 tablespoon chopped fresh parsley leaves*
> *1 pound large shrimp, shelled and deveined*
> *¼ cup dry white wine*
> *2 tablespoons fresh lemon juice*
> *Salt and freshly ground black pepper to taste*

1. In a frying pan, melt the butter over low heat. Sauté the onion, garlic, and parsley until the onion is golden.
2. Add the shrimp. Sauté until the shrimp is just pink. Remove the shrimp to a warmed dish.
3. Add the wine and lemon juice to the pan and simmer for 2 to 3 minutes. Season with salt and pepper. Pour the wine sauce over the shrimp and serve immediately.

YIELD: 4 servings.

Shrimp New Orleans

This spicy Creole dish will be ready in 15 minutes. Serve the shrimp on hot cooked rice.

> *¼ cup butter or margarine*
> *¼ cup chopped onion*
> *¼ cup chopped sweet green pepper*
> *¼ cup diced celery (continued)*

1 garlic clove, minced
1 8-ounce can tomato sauce
½ teaspoon salt
¼ teaspoon dried oregano
¼ teaspoon cayenne pepper
¼ teaspoon dried thyme
Freshly ground black pepper to taste
½ pound shrimp, cooked, shelled, and deveined

1. In a frying pan, melt the butter over medium heat. Sauté the onion, green pepper, celery, and garlic until soft.
2. Add the tomato sauce and seasonings. Simmer, uncovered, over low heat until the sauce thickens, about 5 minutes.
3. Add the shrimp and heat through. Serve immediately.

YIELD: 2 servings.

NOTES: The recipe can be doubled easily.

If raw shrimp is used, sauté it in ¼ cup butter or margarine until pink and firm. Remove from the pan and continue the recipe as written.

Shrimp with Herbed Tomato Sauce

This is a pretty dish that's perfect for the busy hostess. It can be prepared in minutes and needs only a salad, Italian hard rolls, and an excellent bottle of wine to complete the meal.

8 ounces very thin spaghetti
2 tablespoons olive oil
1 garlic clove, minced
1 pound shrimp, shelled and deveined
1 28-ounce can tomatoes in purée, chopped
1 teaspoon dried oregano
1 teaspoon dried basil, or 1 tablespoon chopped fresh basil leaves
Salt and freshly ground black pepper to taste
¼ cup chopped fresh parsley leaves

1. In a saucepan, cook the spaghetti until *al dente*. Drain and set aside.

2. In the same saucepan, heat the oil over medium heat. Sauté the garlic and shrimp until the shrimp turn pink. Remove to a plate.
3. Add all the remaining ingredients except the shrimp and pasta to the saucepan. Cook over low heat for 10 minutes.
4. Add the shrimp and pasta and heat through.

YIELD: 4 servings.

Tuna-Pasta Salad

This main-dish salad should be prepared ahead to allow the flavors to blend. Fix it during the hot summer months.

8 ounces cartwheel pasta
1/2 cup sliced celery
1/2 cup sliced fresh mushrooms
4 green onions (scallions), sliced
1 15-ounce can artichoke hearts, rinsed, drained, and quartered
1 6 1/2-ounce can water-packed albacore tuna, well drained
12 cherry tomatoes, halved
Dijon-Parmesan Dressing (page 169)

1. In a Dutch oven, cook the pasta according to package directions. Drain and chill.
2. Combine all the remaining ingredients with the cooked pasta and toss well. Chill for several hours before serving.

YIELD: 4 to 6 servings.

Hot Garden Pasta

This recipe is a vegetable-lover's delight. It's a pleasant variation of the traditional tomato-based pasta recipes. Serve with garlic bread and a glass of white wine.

8 ounces fettuccine noodles
3 tablespoons olive oil
2 garlic cloves, minced
1/2 teaspoon dried basil *(continued)*

Hot red pepper flakes to taste, optional
Salt and freshly ground black pepper to taste
2 cups chopped broccoli, cooked until just tender, then drained
4 green onions (scallions), sliced
1 pint cherry tomatoes, halved
½ cup grated Parmesan cheese

1. In a large saucepan, cook the pasta until *al dente*. Drain and set aside.
2. In the same pan, heat the oil over medium heat. Sauté the garlic, seasonings, broccoli, and green onions for 2 minutes. Add the pasta, tomatoes, and cheese and toss well. Serve immediately.

YIELD: 2 to 3 servings.

Linguine with White Clam Sauce

This recipe is ready to serve in less than 15 minutes—from start to finish.

8 ounces linguine
1 garlic clove, minced
½ cup olive oil
2 tablespoons minced fresh parsley leaves
¼ teaspoon hot red pepper flakes, optional
1 10-ounce can whole clams, drained

1. In a saucepan or Dutch oven, cook the linguine until *al dente*. Drain and set aside.
2. In the same saucepan, sauté the garlic in the oil until golden. Add the parsley, pepper flakes, and clams. Heat through only.
3. Add the cooked pasta and toss gently. Serve immediately.

YIELD: 4 servings.

Fettuccine Alfredo

This is a restaurant specialty that you can prepare at home for your guests in minutes. Add a light salad and a glass of white wine to complete the menu.

8 ounces egg or spinach fettuccine
2 tablespoons butter or margarine
1 garlic clove, minced
1 cup heavy cream
1 cup grated Parmesan cheese (Freshly grated is best!)
Pinch of ground nutmeg
Salt and freshly ground black pepper to taste
Chopped fresh parsley leaves
Chopped and seeded ripe tomato

1. In a saucepan or Dutch oven, cook the fettuccine until it is *al dente*. Drain and set aside.
2. In the same saucepan, melt the butter over medium-low heat and brown the garlic.
3. Add the cream, cheese, nutmeg, salt and pepper.
4. Add the cooked fettuccine and toss to coat. Serve immediately garnished with the chopped parsley and tomato.

YIELD: 2 servings.

Classic Cheese Fondue

This classic dish can be served as an appetizer or as a main dish. If you have leftover fondue, use it as a delicious sauce over your favorite vegetables.

12 ounces Gruyère cheese, shredded
12 ounces Swiss cheese, shredded
1 teaspoon cornstarch
1 garlic clove
1½ cups dry white wine
Pinch of ground nutmeg
1 loaf French bread, cut into cubes

1. In a bowl, combine the cheeses and cornstarch.
2. In a large saucepan, warm the garlic and wine. Do not boil.
3. Remove the garlic and add the cheese to the saucepan. Heat over low heat until the cheese has melted and the mixture is smooth. Stir in the nutmeg.
4. Transfer to a fondue pot or a heated serving bowl. Serve with the bread cubes as dippers.

YIELD: 4 servings as a main dish; 6 to 8 servings as an appetizer.

SUGGESTED
COMPANY'S COMING MENUS

· *CANDLELIGHT DINNER FOR TWO* ·
Red Wine
Steak Diane (page 125)
Hot Cooked Pasta
Garden Vegetable Salad
Kahlua Custard (page 193)
Beverage

· *A LIGHT LUNCH* ·
Shrimp Curry Bisque (page 54)
Tuna-Pasta Salad (page 137)
Assorted Breads
Marinated Melon (page 188)
Beverage

· *IMPRESS THE CROWD* ·
White Wine
Classic Cheese Fondue (page 139)
Chicken-Artichoke Royal (page 130)
Hot Cooked Pasta
Spinach Salad
Cherries Jubilee (page 184)
Beverage

· *DINNER WITH SPECIAL FRIENDS* ·
White wine
Chicken in Green Peppercorn Sauce (page 128)
Hot Cooked Rice
Tossed Green Salad
Mandarin Chocolate Mousse (page 194)
Beverage

· *DINNER ITALIANO* ·
Marinated Mushrooms (page 164)
White Wine
Shrimp with Herbed Tomato Sauce (page 136)
Italian Salad
Crusty Rolls
Espresso Mousse (page 194)
Beverage

· *FOR THE SOPHISTICATED PALATE* ·
White Wine
Dijon Shrimp Bites (page 162)
Fettuccine Alfredo (page 138)
Mixed Greens
Peach Melba Sundae (page 195)
Beverage

· *MOM AND DAD ARE COMING TO DINNER* ·
Veal Piccata (page 127)
Green Salad
French Bread
Apples in Rum Custard Sauce (page 182)
Beverage

8
Oriental Cookery
The Original ONE BURNER Cuisine

The *one-burner* concept is not a new one, it really began with the Chinese in ancient times. Meats and vegetables were cooked quickly in a single pan designed to fit over a charcoal fire. The ingredients used were sliced and diced in small pieces and cooked quickly in order to conserve precious fuel also needed to heat their dwellings. Out of this necessity for food and fuel conservation, the "stir-fry" method of cooking was born.

Today we may not be as concerned over fuel and food shortages as the Chinese were then, but we are always concerned about time and personal energy shortages. Oriental cookery gives the busy cook a way to combine a potpourri of fresh vegetables and lean meats to produce a flavorful meal in minutes, on *one burner*.

Americans have long savored the individual tastes of meat, potatoes, and vegetables. The Orientals have learned how to combine foods and "marry" the flavors of each. This is truly what makes this cuisine so special and creative. So, whether you like the subtle taste of the Cantonese dishes or the *hot* exciting flavors of the Szechuan, Oriental cookery is the perfect *one-burner* cuisine to fit your busy life-style.

Hints for Successful Oriental Cookery

· Read the entire recipe and measure all ingredients before you begin any cooking.

· Cut all ingredients into uniform sizes to ensure even cooking.

· Partially freeze meats before slicing and dicing. They will be easier to cut.

- For best results, never stir-fry more than 1 pound of meat at a time, whether you're using an electric or traditional wok. It is far better to divide the meat and cook it in two batches.
- Mix cornstarch with a cold liquid ingredient before adding it to the hot wok. If the sauce is mixed ahead of time, be sure to stir the cornstarch back into the liquid, as it tends to settle.
- You may substitute any meats and vegetables for the recommended ingredients. Be careful to use similar amounts and textures so you don't alter the balance of the recipe.
- Use fresh gingerroot when it is called for. There is no dried substitute. Store leftover gingerroot by peeling it and placing it in a small jar filled with dry sherry. Refrigerate.
- Don't overcook stir-fry dishes. Most vegetables should be cooked to the crisp-tender stage. Serve immediately; Chinese dishes do not hold well.

Equipment Needed

Wok, skillet, or large sauté pan with cover

Steaming rack

Cutting board

Cleaver or sharp chef's knife

Spatulas (2)

Grater

DO YOU REALLY NEED A WOK?

You may want to invest in a wok if you are considering doing a lot of stir-frying. The wok does an effective job because of its shape. It is possible to stir-fry in a skillet or large sauté pan, but it's not as easy. Remember that a wok is not a single-purpose appliance. It can be used for sautéing, frying, braising, stewing, and more.

Basic Oriental Grocery Ingredients Needed

Soy sauce—Regular and Dark*

Oil—Peanut and Sesame*

Hoisin sauce*

---

*Available at grocery stores with extensive Oriental foods section or at an Oriental grocery store.

Bouillon granules or broth

Hot red pepper flakes†

Water chestnuts

Bamboo shoots—Canned,
    whole* and sliced

Cornstarch

Garlic

Dry sherry

Gingerroot

Chili paste with garlic* †

Rice

Fungus or dried cloud ears*

Oyster sauce

Quick Wonton Soup

This recipe is a speedy version of the original. No wontons to
fill and fold here!

> *40 frozen meat-filled raviolis*
> *8 cups canned chicken broth*
> *1 tablespoon soy sauce*
> *1 10-ounce package frozen Chinese stir-fry vegetables*
> *4 green onions (scallions), sliced*

1. In a Dutch oven, saucepan, or wok, cook the raviolis according to package directions. Drain.
2. In the same pan, combine all the ingredients except the green
   onions and heat through.
3. Serve in soup bowls and garnish each with green onion
   slices.

YIELD: 6 to 8 servings.

Traditional Wonton Soup

This pretty soup is a wonderful first course to any of the stir-
fried dishes in this chapter. It can be prepared ahead and reheated at the appropriate moment. I have also frozen leftovers
for feasting at a later date.

---

*Available at grocery stores with extensive Oriental foods section or at an
Oriental grocery store.
†For hot spicy dishes!

1 large egg, beaten
1 green onion (scallion), minced
¼ cup minced water chestnuts
1 tablespoon grated fresh gingerroot
1 tablespoon soy sauce
¼ teaspoon salt
Pinch of freshly ground black pepper
½ pound ground fresh pork
1 4½-ounce can small shrimp, drained and minced
40 wonton skins
6 cups canned chicken broth
1 cup very thinly sliced fresh mushrooms
1 cup shredded fresh spinach
¼ pound fresh snow pea pods, sliced diagonally into 1-inch pieces
2 green onions (scallions), sliced, for garnish

1. In a mixing bowl, combine the first 9 ingredients.
2. To fill the wonton skins, place a skin on a work surface with a point toward you. Put 1 heaping teaspoon of the filling just off center, closest to the point nearest you. Fold the point over the filling. Roll over once to cover the filling, leaving a 1-inch tail. Form a circle by grasping the right and left sides. Moisten with a little water and press to seal. (See diagram below.)
3. In a Dutch oven or saucepan, bring 2 quarts of water to a boil. Carefully add the wontons. Lower the heat to a simmer and cook the wontons for 3 minutes.
4. Remove the wontons to a colander and rinse with cold water.
5. In the same pan, bring the chicken broth to a boil. Add the wontons and remaining vegetables except the green onions. Simmer, uncovered, for 3 minutes. Serve in Oriental rice bowls. Garnish each serving with green onions.

YIELD: 8 servings.

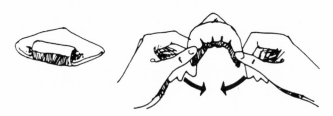

Egg Drop Soup

Prepare this quick recipe as a first course to any of the main dishes in this chapter. If you are using a single burner, don't worry; Chinese cooking is always prepared and eaten in courses.

> *2 14¹/₂-ounce cans chicken broth*
> *1 tablespoon cornstarch, dissolved in 1 tablespoon cold water*
> *2 large eggs, well beaten*
> *2 green onions (scallions), sliced thin*

1. In a saucepan, combine the chicken broth and cornstarch mixture. Heat over medium heat until slightly thickened.
2. Slowly pour in the beaten eggs. Stir only once. Serve immediately, garnishing each serving with the green onion.

YIELD: 4 to 6 servings.

Oriental Hot Pot Soup

Try this American version of an Oriental dish.

> *¹/₂ pound lean ground beef*
> *2 14¹/₂-ounce cans chicken or beef broth*
> *1 10-ounce package frozen Chinese stir-fry vegetables*
> *¹/₂ cup quick-cooking rice*
> *2 green onions (scallions), sliced*
> *1 tablespoon soy sauce*

1. In a saucepan, brown the beef over medium heat. Drain off any excess fat.
2. Combine all the remaining ingredients and add them to the beef. Heat through. The vegetables should be crisp-tender and the rice should be soft.

YIELD: 4 servings.

Hot and Sour Soup

This can be a whole-meal soup or a first course. Serve it from a pretty tureen right at the table. For convenience, prepare it ahead and reheat it when ready to serve.

Boiling water
4 dried black mushrooms
2 dried cloud ears (fungus)
¼ pound boneless pork tenderloin, cut into matchsticks
1 teaspoon cornstarch
2 tablespoons vegetable or peanut oil
6 cups canned chicken broth
½ cup bamboo shoots, cut into matchsticks
2 tablespoons soy sauce
¼ teaspoon hot red pepper flakes, or to taste
⅓ cup white vinegar
2 tablespoons cornstarch, dissolved in ¼ cup cold water
8 ounces bean curd (tofu), cut into thin strips
2 large eggs, beaten
1 tablespoon sesame oil
2 green onions (scallions), sliced, for garnish

1. Pour boiling water over mushrooms and cloud ears in separate bowls. Let stand for 2 hours. Then remove the stems and woody parts.
2. Thinly slice the mushrooms and cloud ears.
3. Mix the pork and the teaspoon of cornstarch together in a bowl.
4. Preheat a wok or Dutch oven over high heat. Add the vegetable oil. Stir-fry the pork until it turns white. Add the chicken broth, mushrooms, cloud ears, bamboo shoots, soy sauce, pepper flakes, vinegar, and cornstarch mixture.
5. Add the bean curd and bring to a boil; then turn off the heat. Add the beaten egg and stir once. Then add the sesame oil.
6. Serve, or refrigerate until ready to reheat. Garnish each serving with sliced green onions.

YIELD: 6 to 8 servings.

Pepper and Tomato Steak

This colorful recipe has all the requirements for a perfect after-work meal when it is served with hot cooked rice or chow mein noodles.

½ cup cold water
1 tablespoon cornstarch
¼ cup soy sauce
2 tablespoons brown sugar
2 tablespoons vegetable or peanut oil
1 pound round or flank steak, cut into thin strips across the grain
2 sweet green peppers, cut into thin strips
2 medium-size ripe tomatoes, cut into wedges

1. Combine the water, cornstarch, soy sauce, and sugar in a bowl. Set aside.
2. Preheat a skillet or wok over high heat. Add the oil and sauté the beef and green peppers until the beef is no longer pink.
3. Push the beef to the sides of the pan and add the cornstarch mixture. Stir and cook until thickened.
4. Stir in the tomatoes and heat through. Serve immediately.

YIELD: 4 to 6 servings.

Beef with Snow Peas

In just 2 minutes this dish is ready to serve. Pass the chow mein noodles or fluffy hot rice.

2 tablespoons soy sauce
2 tablespoons oyster sauce
1 tablespoon dry sherry
½ teaspoon sugar
¼ cup canned beef broth
2 teaspoons cornstarch, dissolved in 1 tablespoon cold water
2 tablespoons vegetable or peanut oil
1 pound flank steak, sliced thin against the grain
½ pound snow peas, trim and strings removed
1 8-ounce can sliced water chestnuts, drained

1. Combine the first 6 ingredients in a bowl. Set aside.
2. Heat a wok or skillet over high heat. Add the oil and stir-fry the steak until it is no longer pink.
3. Add the snow peas and water chestnuts and stir-fry for 1 minute.
4. Add the soy sauce mixture and stir and cook until thickened. Serve immediately.

YIELD: 4 servings.

Oriental Beef and Vegetables

This classic recipe can be prepared for under 300 calories per serving!

>*3/4 pound round steak*
>*1/2 teaspoon instant beef bouillon granules*
>*1/3 cup hot water*
>*2 tablespoons soy sauce*
>*1 tablespoon vegetable or peanut oil*
>*1 garlic clove, minced*
>*2 teaspoons grated fresh gingerroot*
>*4 green onions (scallions), sliced*
>*2 carrots, peeled and sliced thin*
>*1 cup diagonally sliced celery*
>*1 cup sliced fresh mushrooms*
>*6 cups fresh whole spinach leaves, washed,*
>　　*drained, and with stems removed*

1. Partially freeze the beef; then slice it into thin strips.
2. Combine the bouillon granules, water, and soy sauce in a bowl. Set aside.
3. Heat a wok or skillet over high heat. Add the oil and stir-fry the garlic and gingerroot until lightly browned.
4. Add the onions, carrots, celery, and mushrooms. Stir-fry for 2 minutes. Remove the vegetables to a platter.
5. Add the meat to the pan. Stir-fry until it is no longer pink. Add the soy sauce mixture and heat through.
6. Return the vegetables to the pan. Add the spinach, cover, and cook for 1 minute. Serve immediately.

YIELD: 4 servings.

NOTE: Substitute any of your favorite vegetables for those recommended above.

Mongolian Beef

This dish is especially pretty because of the "matchstick" shapes. Serve it with hot cooked rice.

> *1 pound broccoli flowerets*
> *2 tablespoons vegetable or peanut oil*
> *1 pound flank steak, cut into matchsticks*
> *½ cup bamboo shoots, cut into matchsticks*
> *6 green onions (scallions), cut into 1-inch pieces*

SAUCE

> *2 tablespoons dry sherry*
> *¼ cup hoisin sauce*
> *¼ cup dark soy sauce*
> *¼ cup canned chicken broth*
> *½ teaspoon sugar*
> *1 tablespoon cornstarch*
> *1 teaspoon chili paste with garlic, optional*

1. Steam the broccoli until it is crisp-tender. Set aside.
2. Combine the sauce ingredients in a bowl. Set aside.
3. Heat a wok or skillet over high heat. Add the oil. Stir-fry the meat until it is just pink.
4. Add the bamboo shoots and onions. Stir-fry for 1 minute.
5. Stir the sauce mixture and add it to the pan. Cook and stir until thickened.
6. Place the meat mixture on a platter and garnish with a ring of broccoli flowerets. Serve immediately.

YIELD: 4 servings.

Marinated Korean Beef

Serve with hot cooked rice and a mixed fruit salad for dessert.

> *2 green onions (scallions), sliced thin*
> *2 tablespoons soy sauce*
> *1 tablespoon sesame oil*
> *½ teaspoon sugar*

    1 garlic clove, minced
    Hot pepper sauce to taste
    1 pound beef flank steak, sliced thin against the grain
    Vegetable or peanut oil for deep-fat frying

DIPPING SAUCE

    3 tablespoons soy sauce
    2 tablespoons dry sherry
    2 teaspoons sugar
    1 tablespoon water
    1 green onion (scallion), sliced thin
    1 teaspoon sesame oil
    Dash of hot pepper sauce

1. Combine the onions, soy sauce, sesame oil, sugar, garlic, and hot pepper sauce in a bowl. Add the beef and marinate for 30 minutes.
2. To make the Dipping Sauce, combine all the ingredients in a bowl.
3. In a wok or skillet, heat a 1-inch depth of oil to 375 degrees. Fry a handful of the meat strips at a time until lightly browned. Remove to paper towels and keep warm. Repeat until all the meat strips are cooked. Serve with the Dipping Sauce.

YIELD: 4 servings.

Easy Cantonese Pork

This is the perfect recipe for the novice cook or for the children. Serve with chow mein noodles.

    1 tablespoon vegetable or peanut oil
    1 pound pork tenderloin, cut into matchsticks
    ½ cup sliced fresh mushrooms
    1 small onion, sliced
    2 cups diagonally sliced celery
    1 10½-ounce can mushroom gravy
    1 tablespoon soy sauce
    Pinch of freshly ground black pepper
    1 16-ounce can bean sprouts, drained

1. Heat a wok or skillet over high heat. Add the oil. Stir-fry the meat until it is firm and white.
2. Add the mushrooms and onion. Stir-fry for 2 minutes.
3. Add the celery, gravy, soy sauce, and pepper. Lower the heat, cover, and simmer for 30 minutes. Add the bean sprouts and heat through.

YIELD: 4 to 6 servings.

Pork and Peppers

There are just a few ingredients in this recipe, but it's pretty and very flavorful. The egg white and the cornstarch coats the meat with a shiny glaze. Serve this dish with chow mein noodles or hot cooked rice.

> *½ pound boneless lean pork, cut into matchsticks*
> *1 teaspoon cornstarch*
> *1 large egg white*
> *2 tablespoons vegetable or peanut oil*
> *1 sweet green pepper, cut into matchsticks*
> *1 sweet red pepper, cut into matchsticks*
> *1 tablespoon dry sherry*
> *1 tablespoon soy sauce*

1. Combine the pork, cornstarch, and egg white in a bowl. Mix well.
2. Heat a wok or skillet over high heat. Add the oil. Stir-fry the pork until it is firm and white.
3. Add the peppers, stir-fry for 1 minute.
4. Sprinkle with the sherry and soy sauce and heat through. Serve immediately.

YIELD: 4 servings.

Lamb and Lettuce Packets

You'll love this unusual Chinese dish that wraps a lettuce leaf around a stir-fried lamb mixture.

2 tablespoons canned beef broth
2 tablespoons dry sherry
2 tablespoons soy sauce
1 tablespoon cornstarch
2 tablespoons vegetable or peanut oil
1 pound boneless lamb, cut into thin strips across the grain
2 teaspoons grated fresh gingerroot
$^{1}/_{2}$ cup fresh bean sprouts
2 green onions (scallions), sliced
16 medium-size romaine, Bibb, or iceberg lettuce leaves

PLUM DIPPING SAUCE

$^{2}/_{3}$ cup plum preserves
1 tablespoon hoisin sauce
1 tablespoon soy sauce
1 teaspoon grated fresh gingerroot

1. Combine the beef broth, sherry, soy sauce, and cornstarch in a small bowl. Set aside.
2. Combine all the ingredients for the Plum Dipping Sauce in a bowl and mix well. Set aside.
3. Heat a wok or skillet over high heat. Add the oil. Stir-fry the lamb until tender, about 3 minutes. Remove to a platter.
4. Stir-fry the gingerroot, bean sprouts, and onions for 1 minute. Return the lamb to the pan.
5. Stir the sherry sauce mixture and add it to the pan. Cook and stir until thickened.
6. Fill the lettuce leaves with a few tablespoons of the lamb mixture and fold envelope style. Serve immediately with the Plum Dipping Sauce.

YIELD: 4 servings.

Chicken and Peanuts

This is a classic Szechuan dish that will please those who like it HOT! Serve with rice.

SAUCE

> 2 tablespoons dark soy sauce
> 1 tablespoon dry sherry
> 1 teaspoon sugar
> 1/4 cup canned chicken broth
> 1 teaspoon cornstarch
> 1 teaspoon sesame oil

2 tablespoons vegetable or peanut oil
1 pound skinned and boned chicken breasts, cut into 1/2-inch cubes
1/2 cup blanched unsalted peanuts
5 to 10 dried whole red chile peppers
1 6- or 8-ounce can whole water chestnuts, drained and diced
4 green onions (scallions), cut into 1/2-inch diagonal pieces
2 garlic cloves, minced

1. Combine the sauce ingredients in a bowl and set aside.
2. Heat a wok or skillet over high heat. Add the oil. Stir-fry the chicken for 2 to 4 minutes, or until cooked. Remove to a plate.
3. Stir-fry the peanuts for 1 minute, or until golden brown. Remove to a small bowl.
4. Stir-fry the chile peppers, water chestnuts, onions, and garlic for 1 to 2 minutes. Add additional oil, if necessary. Return the chicken to the wok.
5. Stir the sauce and add it to the chicken mixture. Cook and stir until thickened. Add the peanuts. *Discard the chile peppers* and serve immediately.

YIELD: 4 to 6 servings.

Chicken and Green Peppers

This spicy dish can be prepared without the red pepper if you want to tone down the hot taste. Rice is delicious with this entrée.

> 3 tablespoons soy sauce
> 2 teaspoons cornstarch
> 2 tablespoons dry sherry

1 garlic clove, minced
1 teaspoon grated fresh gingerroot
1 teaspoon sugar
1/4 to 1/2 teaspoon hot red pepper flakes, optional
2 tablespoons vegetable or peanut oil
2 sweet green peppers, cut into 1/2-inch pieces
4 green onions (scallions), cut into 1-inch diagonal
   pieces
1 cup walnut halves
1 pound skinned and boned chicken breasts, cut into
   1-inch cubes

1. Combine the soy sauce, cornstarch, sherry, garlic, ginger-root, sugar, and hot pepper flakes in a bowl. Set aside.
2. Heat a wok or skillet over high heat. Add the oil. Stir-fry the green peppers and onions for 1 minute. Remove to a plate.
3. Add the walnuts to the wok and stir-fry for 1 minute, or until golden brown. Remove to the plate with the peppers.
4. Add additional oil to the wok if necessary and stir-fry the chicken for 2 to 4 minutes, or until it is cooked. Return all the ingredients to the pan.
5. Stir the soy mixture and then pour it into the chicken mixture. Cook and stir until thickened. Serve immediately.

YIELD: 4 to 6 servings.

Chicken and Button Mushrooms (Moo Goo Gai Pan)

This recipe requires very little preparation, which makes it perfect for busy days. Serve with rice or chow mein noodles.

3/4 pound skinned and boned chicken breasts, cut into 1/2-inch cubes
2 teaspoons cornstarch
1/2 teaspoon salt
Pinch of freshly ground black pepper
1 4-ounce can button mushrooms, drained and 1/4 cup liquid reserved
1 tablespoon cornstarch
2 tablespoons vegetable or peanut oil
1 garlic clove, minced (continued)

2 teaspoons grated fresh gingerroot
¼ cup toasted blanched almonds

1. Dredge the chicken in a mixture of the 2 teaspoons cornstarch, salt, and pepper. Set aside.
2. Combine the reserved mushroom liquid and the 1 tablespoon cornstarch. Set aside.
3. Heat a wok or skillet over high heat. Add the oil. Stir-fry
   the chicken, garlic, and gingerroot for 2 to 4 minutes, or
   until the chicken is cooked.
4. Add the mushrooms and heat through. Add the mushroom
   liquid mixture, stir, and cook until thickened. Garnish with
   the toasted almonds and serve immediately.

YIELD: 4 servings.

Mix and Match Chicken Stir-Fry

This is the kind of dish that can use any combination of fresh
vegetables available in season. Serve over hot cooked rice or
chow mein noodles.

SAUCE

> 1 pound skinned and boned chicken breasts, cut
>   into ¾-inch cubes
> 1 pound vegetables, cut into similar shapes and
>   sizes for even cooking
> 1 garlic clove, minced
> 1 tablespoon grated fresh gingerroot
> 2 tablespoons dry sherry
> 1 tablespoon soy sauce
> ½ teaspoon sugar
> ½ cup canned chicken broth
> 2 teaspoons cornstarch
> 2 tablespoons vegetable or peanut oil

1. Combine the sauce ingredients in a bowl. Set aside.

2. Heat a wok or skillet over high heat. Add the oil. Stir-fry the chicken for 2 to 4 minutes, or until it is cooked. Remove to a plate.
3. Stir-fry the vegetables, garlic, and gingerroot for 2 minutes. Return the chicken to the wok.
4. Stir the sauce and add it to the chicken mixture. Cook and stir until thickened. Serve immediately.

YIELD: 4 to 6 servings.

Shrimp in Red Sauce

In less than 10 minutes this dish is ready to serve. Prepare the rice first and keep it warm in a covered bowl. Serve a fruit salad for dessert for a quick, but very elegant, meal.

> *2 tablespoons vegetable or peanut oil*
> *1 pound fresh or frozen shrimp, shelled and deveined*
> *1 garlic clove, minced*
> *2 teaspoons grated fresh gingerroot*
> *3 tablespoons catsup*
> *1 tablespoon soy sauce*
> *1 tablespoon dry sherry*
> *1 teaspoon sugar*
> *Dash of hot pepper sauce*

1. Heat a wok or skillet over high heat. Add the oil. Stir-fry the shrimp until they are pink, about 2 minutes.
2. Add all the remaining ingredients and heat to boiling. Serve immediately.

YIELD: 4 servings.

Stir-Fried Shrimp and Lettuce

This is a typically Chinese recipe—very good and low in calories! Delicious served over boiled rice.

> *½ pound shrimp, shelled and deveined*
> *1 tablespoon cornstarch (continued)*

2 tablespoons vegetable or peanut oil
2 teaspoons grated fresh gingerroot
1 garlic clove, minced
1 head iceberg lettuce, shredded
Salt to taste
¼ cup canned chicken broth

1. Toss the shrimp with the cornstarch to coat them.
2. Heat a wok or skillet over high heat. Add the oil. Stir-fry the shrimp, gingerroot, and garlic until the shrimp turn pink, about 2 minutes.
3. Add the lettuce and stir-fry for 1 minute.
4. Stir in the chicken broth and heat through. Serve immediately.

YIELD: 2 to 4 servings.

Curried Shrimp

This shrimp is a bit spicy, but that can be adjusted by the amount of curry powder used. Serve with rice.

2 teaspoons cornstarch
2 teaspoons cold water
1 to 3 teaspoons curry powder
½ teaspoon sugar
½ teaspoon salt
½ cup canned chicken broth
1 tablespoon dry sherry
2 tablespoons vegetable or peanut oil
1 pound fresh or frozen shrimp, shelled and deveined
1 large onion, sliced

1. Combine the cornstarch, water, curry powder, sugar, salt, chicken broth, and sherry in a bowl. Set aside.
2. Heat a wok or skillet over high heat. Add the oil. Stir-fry the shrimp and onion until the shrimp turn pink, about 2 minutes.
3. Add the sauce mixture, stir, and cook until thickened. Serve immediately.

YIELD: 4 servings.

Egg Foo Yung

You've enjoyed this favorite at Chinese restaurants, so why not prepare it at home? Cook it in deep fat in a skillet or wok or fry on a griddle. Serve with the sauce and hot cooked rice.

> *6 large eggs*
> *1 cup fresh bean sprouts*
> *2 green onions (scallions), sliced thin*
> *1 4½-ounce can small shrimp, drained*
> *Vegetable oil*

SAUCE

> *2 cups water*
> *⅓ cup soy sauce*
> *2 tablespoons cornstarch*
> *1 tablespoon sugar*

1. Beat the eggs lightly and combine with all the ingredients except the oil.
2. Combine all the sauce ingredients in a saucepan and cook over medium heat until thickened. Stir constantly. Keep warm while preparing the patties.
3. Grease a griddle or skillet and heat over medium heat.
4. Drop ¼ cup of the egg mixture for each patty on the hot surface. Turn when browned. Repeat until all the patties are cooked. Serve with the sauce.

YIELD: 6 servings.

VARIATION—Deep-fat Method
   The mixture may be cooked in deep fat as is done in restaurants. Carefully drop each patty in 2 inches of oil heated in a skillet or wok to 375 degrees. Turn when browned.

Chinese Fried Rice

Use leftover meats and rice to create this excellent entrée. The cooked rice must be chilled before preparing this recipe to achieve the desired consistency.

2 tablespoons vegetable or peanut oil
2 large eggs, beaten
1/2 cup diced ham, shrimp, or pork
1 garlic clove, minced
1 teaspoon grated fresh gingerroot
2 green onions (scallions), sliced thin
4 cups rice, chilled
3 tablespoons soy sauce

1. Heat a wok or skillet over high heat. Add 1 tablespoon of the oil. Add the eggs and cook without stirring until they are set. Remove the eggs to a plate and cut them into thin strips. Set aside.
2. Add the remaining oil to the pan. Stir-fry the meat, garlic, gingerroot, onion, rice, and soy sauce for 2 minutes, or until heated through.
3. Add the egg strips and toss to combine. Serve immediately.

YIELD: 4 servings.

SUGGESTED ORIENTAL COOKERY MENUS

· *BUSY COOKS' MENU* ·
Shrimp in Red Sauce (page 157)
Hot Cooked Rice
Marinated Melon (page 188)
Hot Chinese Tea

· *JUST LIKE THE RESTAURANT MENU* ·
Traditional Wonton Soup (page 144)
Beef with Snow Peas (page 148)
Chow Mein Noodles
Almond Cookies   Fortune Cookies
Hot Chinese Tea

· *AFTER-WORK MENU* ·
Pork and Peppers (page 152)
Chow Mein Noodles or Hot Cooked Rice
Marinated Melon (page 188)
Hot Chinese Tea

· *MARATHON CHINESE DINNER FOR GUESTS* ·
Rice Wine
Hot and Sour Soup (page 147)
Curried Shrimp (page 158)
Chicken and Button Mushrooms (page 155)
Mongolian Beef (page 150)
Hot Cooked Rice
Sorbet
Almond Cookies   Fortune Cookies
Hot Chinese Tea

· *LEAN STIR-FRY DINNER* ·
Egg Drop Soup (page 146)
Mix and Match Chicken Stir-Fry (page 156)
Shredded Lettuce
Sherbet
Hot Chinese Tea

9
Side-Dish Showstoppers
Pulling It All Together

Now that you have selected the entrée, it's time to complete the menu and pull it all together. Serve an appetizer, add a salad, prepare a special sauce, or whatever strikes your fancy. Use this chapter as little or as much as you want, depending on the complexity of the meal you are planning. Remember that the rule of simplicity still applies, but if you're looking for a special salad dressing or a great after-dinner coffee, this is the chapter to consult.

Appetizers

Dijon Shrimp Bites

This is a departure from the popular rumaki and perfect when you want an elegant hot appetizer.

> *12 slices bacon*
> *Dijon mustard*
> *24 medium-size shrimp, shelled and deveined*

1. Cut each slice of bacon in half. Spread the bacon with mustard.
2. Place a shrimp on each slice of bacon, wrap, and secure with a toothpick.
3. Put the wrapped shrimp in a skillet. Cook over medium heat until the bacon is crisp and the shrimp are cooked, about 7 minutes. Serve immediately.

YIELD: 24 appetizers.

Chicken Wing Appetizers

Prepare these chicken wings a day ahead to give the flavors a chance to blend.

> *3 pounds chicken wings, wing tips discarded*
> *1 cup honey*
> *½ cup soy sauce*
> *2 tablespoons catsup*
> *1 teaspoon sesame oil*
> *1 garlic clove, minced*
> *1 teaspoon grated fresh gingerroot*
> *2 tablespoons toasted sesame seeds*
> *2 green onions (scallions), sliced thin*

1. Divide each chicken wing into 2 pieces by cutting between the joints.
2. Combine the first 7 ingredients in a Dutch oven or wok. Cover and bring to a boil. Lower the heat and simmer for 1 hour. Cool to room temperature; then cover and refrigerate. Reheat when ready to serve.
3. Serve on a large platter or in a chafing dish. Garnish the wings with the toasted sesame seeds and sliced green onions.

YIELD: 8 to 10 servings.

Chili con Queso

No advanced preparation is needed for this spicy appetizer. Simply heat the ingredients and serve in a pretty earthenware bowl surrounded with tortilla chips.

> *1 15-ounce can chili without beans*
> *2 8-ounce packages cream cheese, softened*
> *2 cups shredded Cheddar cheese*
> *1 4-ounce can diced chiles, drained*
> *Tortilla chips or corn chips*

In a saucepan or fondue pot, combine all the ingredients except the tortilla chips. Cook over medium-low heat until well blended, stirring often. Serve with the tortilla chips as dippers.

YIELD: 6 servings.

Saganaki

I first tasted this delicious appetizer at a Greek restaurant in Chicago. I now prepare it at home with great panache.

> *1 large egg, beaten*
> *1 teaspoon all-purpose flour*
> *¾ pound kasseri cheese, cut into 1-inch squares*
> *¼ cup butter or margarine*
> *2 tablespoons brandy*
> *1 lemon, halved*

1. Combine the egg and flour in a bowl. Dip the cheese squares into the flour mixture.
2. In a frying pan, melt the butter over medium-high heat. Sauté the cheese on all sides until soft and lightly browned.
3. Add the brandy to the pan and ignite it with a long match. When the flame subsides, squeeze the lemon over the cheese. Serve immediately.

YIELD: 8 servings.

Marinated Mushrooms

Prepare the mushrooms ahead and serve as an unusually tasty appetizer with cocktail picks or as a salad on a bed of shredded lettuce.

> *⅔ cup olive oil*
> *½ cup water*
> *½ cup fresh lemon juice*
> *½ teaspoon salt*
> *2 garlic cloves*
> *1 bay leaf*
> *½ teaspoon freshly ground black pepper*
> *1 pound medium-size fresh mushrooms*
> *Chopped fresh parsley leaves*

1. In a saucepan, combine all the ingredients except the mushrooms and chopped parsley. Cover and bring to a boil over medium heat. Lower the heat and simmer for 15 minutes.

2. Skim off all the whole spices and discard them.
3. Add the mushrooms to the pan and simmer for 5 minutes. Pour into a bowl, cover, and chill for several hours or overnight.
4. Drain, garnish with freshly chopped parsley, and serve with cocktail picks.

YIELD: 8 servings.

French Fried Eggplant Strips

This is a perfect recipe to enjoy with a cocktail and good conversation before dinner. Prepare the recipe ahead to the point of deep-frying and refrigerate until you're ready to cook. Then it becomes easy for any host or hostess to handle.

1 large egg
2 tablespoons water
½ cup seasoned bread crumbs
½ cup grated Parmesan cheese
1 teaspoon salt
¼ teaspoon paprika
1 large eggplant, peeled and cut into 3- by ⅜- by ⅜-inch strips
Vegetable oil for deep-frying

1. Beat the egg and water together in a shallow bowl.
2. In a second bowl combine the bread crumbs, cheese, salt, and paprika.
3. Dip the eggplant strips into the egg mixture; then dip them in the crumb mixture. Chill on a baking sheet for at least 1 hour.
4. In a Dutch oven or deep-fat fryer, heat the oil to 400 degrees. Fry a few strips of eggplant at a time until they are golden brown. Drain on paper towels and serve as soon as possible.

YIELD: 6 servings.

Salads and Salad Dressings

Parmesan-Romaine Salad

Serve this light salad with just about any entrée. You'll find this one will become a basic in your guest menu. If possible, shred the cheese right before serving for the best flavor and crisp appearance.

1 garlic clove
¼ teaspoon salt
2 tablespoons Dijon mustard
2 tablespoons tarragon vinegar
⅓ to ½ cup olive oil
1 large head romaine lettuce, cut into long, thin shreds and patted
  dry with paper towels
⅓ cup roasted salted pine nuts
⅓ cup finely shredded Parmesan cheese

1. In a salad bowl, mash the garlic clove and rub it over the entire inner surface of the bowl.
2. Whisk together the salt, mustard, and vinegar. Add the oil in a steady stream until the dressing is thickened and emulsified.
3. Toss in the romaine and pine nuts and toss well to coat.
4. Serve on individual salad plates, topped with the finely shredded cheese.

YIELD: 4 to 6 servings.

NOTE: Roasted pine nuts are available in specialty nut shops.

Marinated Vegetables in Vinaigrette

When there is no time to fuss over a salad, this is the answer. Toss this together the day before and let the flavors blend.

1½ quarts of your favorite sliced raw vegetables (celery, carrots,
  cauliflower, broccoli, zucchini, mushrooms, green beans, green
  onions, etc.)
1 cup olive oil

⅓ cup fresh lemon juice
1 garlic clove, minced
Salt and freshly ground black pepper
2 tablespoons chopped fresh basil leaves

1. Choose a variety of fresh vegetables of your choice. Cut them into bite-size pieces. Blanch them in boiling water for 1 minute. Drain and cool.
2. In a shallow bowl, beat the oil, lemon juice, garlic, salt, and pepper until thickened.
3. Pour the dressing over the vegetables. Toss to coat. Chill overnight in a covered container.
4. Just before serving toss the vegetables with the fresh basil.

YIELD: 6 to 8 servings.

Frozen Slaw

Keep this salad in the freezer for those days when you don't even have the time to put a simple green salad together.

1 medium-size head green cabbage, shredded
1 teaspoon salt
1 small onion, chopped
½ sweet green pepper, diced
1 cup white vinegar
⅓ cup water
2 cups sugar
1½ teaspoons celery seeds
1 teaspoon mustard seeds

1. Sprinkle the cabbage with the salt and let it stand for 1 hour. Drain off the liquid and squeeze the cabbage dry. Add the onion and green pepper.
2. In a saucepan, combine the vinegar, water, sugar, celery and mustard seeds and bring to a boil. Boil for 2 minutes.
3. Pour the dressing over the cabbage mixture and cool.
4. Pack into serving-size freezing containers or freezer bags and seal.
5. Thaw when ready to serve and serve cold.

YIELD: 6 to 8 servings.

Pesto Potato Salad

What could be easier and more flavorful than tossing hot cooked potatoes with Pesto Sauce for a quick salad idea?

> *2½ pounds unpeeled new red potatoes*
> *1 recipe Pesto Sauce (following recipe)*
> *Salt to taste*

1. Cook the potatoes in boiling water until they are tender but firm. Slice while warm.
2. Toss carefully with the Pesto Sauce and season with salt. Serve immediately.

YIELD: 6 to 8 servings.

Pesto Sauce

If you like garlic and Parmesan cheese, this is a great new sauce experience to try. Toss this flavorful sauce with hot cooked pasta, add it to an omelet, stir it into cooked rice or tomato sauces, or add it to mayonnaise or whatever else strikes your fancy. You'll soon find many creative uses of your own.

> *2 cups fresh spinach or parsley leaves*
> *2 large fresh garlic cloves*
> *½ cup walnuts*
> *1 cup olive oil*
> *1 tablespoon dried basil*
> *½ cup grated Parmesan cheese*
> *Salt and freshly ground black pepper to taste*

1. In a blender or food processor, combine all the ingredients. Cover and process until a smooth paste forms.
2. Transfer to a covered container and refrigerate until ready to use.

YIELD: 1½ cups.

Dijon-Parmesan Dressing

⅓ *cup olive oil*
2 tablespoons Dijon mustard
1 tablespoon tarragon vinegar
1 tablespoon fresh lemon juice
⅓ *cup grated Parmesan cheese*
1 garlic clove, minced
¼ *teaspoon salt*
Pinch of freshly ground black pepper

Combine all the ingredients in a bowl and blend well.

YIELD: 1 cup.

Peppercorn Dressing

This is a pungent dressing that can be served on just plain greens and still be spectacular.

¾ *cup sour cream*
¼ *cup mayonnaise*
2 tablespoons milk
1 tablespoon Dijon mustard
1 tablespoon fresh lemon juice
1 tablespoon freshly cracked black peppercorns
Pinch of garlic salt
Pinch of curry powder

Combine all the ingredients in a bowl and mix well. Cover and chill for several hours before serving.

YIELD: 1¼ cups.

Poppy Seed Dressing

An unusual dressing for spinach greens or fruit salads.

> *1 large egg*
> *¹/₂ cup sugar*
> *2 teaspoons powdered mustard*
> *1 teaspoon salt*
> *¹/₂ cup white vinegar*
> *2 tablespoons finely grated onion*
> *1¹/₂ cups vegetable oil*
> *2 tablespoons poppy seeds*

1. In a blender container, combine the egg, sugar, mustard, salt, vinegar, and onion. Cover and process at medium speed. Then, while blending, add the oil in a steady stream.
2. Transfer the dressing to a container and stir in the poppy seeds. Cover and refrigerate until ready to use.

YIELD: 2¹/₂ cups.

Yogurt-Herb Dressing

> *¹/₂ cup plain yogurt*
> *¹/₂ cup sour cream*
> *1 green onion (scallion), sliced thin*
> *1 garlic clove, minced*
> *¹/₂ teaspoon dried oregano*
> *¹/₄ teaspoon crushed dried mint*
> *Pinch of salt and freshly ground black pepper*

Combine all the ingredients in a bowl and mix well. Cover and chill until ready to serve.

YIELD: 1 cup.

Rice, Pasta, and Bread

Wild Rice with Mushrooms

The nutty taste of wild rice is a very nice addition to chicken and fish entrées.

> *1 cup wild rice*
> *3 cups water*
> *1 teaspoon salt*
> *2 tablespoons butter or margarine*
> *¼ pound fresh mushrooms, sliced*

1. Rinse the rice in a colander under cool running water until the water runs clean. Remove any foreign particles.
2. In a saucepan, bring the water and salt to a boil over high heat. Add the rice, cover, and simmer for 45 to 50 minutes, or until the rice is tender. Add additional water, if necessary. Transfer the rice to a serving bowl and keep it warm.
3. In the same saucepan, melt the butter over medium heat. Sauté the mushrooms for 3 minutes. Stir the mushrooms and butter into the cooked rice.
4. Cover with aluminum foil to keep warm or serve immediately.

YIELD: 4 to 6 servings.

Buttered Green Rice

This easy side dish is pretty and flavorful to serve with fish, chicken, and veal.

> *3 cups hot cooked rice*
> *3 tablespoons butter or margarine*
> *¼ cup sliced green onions (scallions)*
> *⅓ cup chopped fresh parsley leaves*
> *⅓ cup chopped fresh spinach leaves*
> *Salt and freshly ground black pepper to taste*

Combine all the ingredients and toss carefully. Serve immediately.

YIELD: 4 servings.

Poppy Seed Noodles

When your recipe calls for cooked buttered noodles, try adding poppy seeds just before serving. This recipe is especially good with beef stew.

> *6 cups cooked pasta*
> *3 tablespoons butter or margarine*
> *1 tablespoon poppy seeds*

1. Cook pasta according to package directions; then drain.
2. In a frying pan, melt the butter over medium heat. Add the cooked pasta and poppy seeds and toss and heat through. Serve immediately.

YIELD: 6 servings.

Egg Drop Dumplings

Add this hearty finishing touch to your favorite soup.

> *2 large eggs*
> *¹/₂ cup all-purpose flour*
> *¹/₂ teaspoon salt*
> *Pinch of ground nutmeg*
> *Pinch of freshly ground black pepper*
> *¹/₃ cup butter or margarine, softened*

1. In a small bowl, beat the eggs. Add the flour, seasonings, and butter.
2. Drop the batter by the teaspoonful into boiling soup. Cook for 5 minutes.

YIELD: 6 to 8 servings.

Parsley Drop Dumplings

Drop this basic dumpling into stew to add a country flavor and to make it a complete dish.

2 cups all-purpose flour
1 tablespoon baking powder
1/2 teaspoon salt
1/4 cup finely chopped fresh parsley leaves
Pinch of ground nutmeg
Pinch of freshly ground black pepper
2 tablespoons butter or margarine
1/2 to 3/4 cup boiling water

1. Sift the flour, baking powder, and salt into a mixing bowl. Add the seasonings.
2. Add the butter and boiling water and stir to form a thick batter.
3. Drop the batter by the tablespoonful into boiling stew. Lower the heat to a simmer and cook, covered, for 10 minutes.

YIELD: 8 servings.

Soup and Salad Croutons

Nothing tops a salad or a bowl of homemade soup better than well-seasoned, crisp croutons. Make these when you have stale bread and keep them in an airtight container until ready to use.

1/2 cup butter or margarine
2 tablespoons olive oil
4 cups stale bread (white, rye, sourdough), cut into cubes
2 garlic cloves, minced
1 1/2 teaspoons dried tarragon, basil, or parsley
1/4 cup grated Parmesan cheese

1. In a frying pan, heat the butter and oil over medium-low heat.
2. Add the bread cubes and cook, stirring constantly until well coated with the butter.
3. Turn the heat to low and add the garlic and herbs. Toss to coat the bread cubes. Cook and stir occasionally until the cubes are lightly browned, about 20 minutes.
4. Remove the croutons to a storage container and toss with the cheese. Cool and then cover.

YIELD: 4 cups.

No-Oven Bacon Corn Bread

This corn bread is baked on top of the stove. It's perfect for people who don't have ovens or for people who don't want to overheat their apartments. Serve it with one of the many soups in this book.

> 1 cup all-purpose flour
> 4 teaspoons baking powder
> 1/4 cup sugar
> 1/2 teaspoon salt
> 1 cup yellow or white cornmeal
> 1 large egg, slightly beaten
> 1/4 cup butter or margarine, melted
> 1 cup milk
> 1/3 cup crumbled cooked bacon

1. Sift the dry ingredients together.
2. Combine the egg, butter, and milk in a mixing bowl.
3. Gently combine dry and liquid ingredients only until blended. Add the bacon.
4. Heat a 9-inch skillet over low heat. Spray with vegetable cooking spray. Pour the batter into the skillet, cover, and cook over low heat until done, about 25 to 30 minutes. When done, the corn bread will spring back when touched with a fingertip.

YIELD: 8 to 10 servings.

Sandwich Mustards

Sweet and Spicy Mustard Spread

Serve as a spread or a sauce with ham or pork.

> 2 tablespoons powdered mustard
> 1 tablespoon white vinegar
> 1 cup orange marmalade or apricot preserves

1. In a small bowl, combine the mustard and vinegar. Let stand for 15 minutes. Stir in the marmalade.

YIELD: 1 cup.

Coarse Horseradish Mustard

A perfect spread for your favorite sandwich.

> *¹/₂ cup yellow mustard seeds*
> *1 cup dry white wine, warmed*
> *¹/₂ cup white vinegar, warmed*
> *1 tablespoon prepared horseradish*
> *2 teaspoons honey*
> *¹/₂ teaspoon salt*

1. In a small bowl, combine the mustard seeds, wine, and vinegar. Cover and let stand at room temperature overnight.
2. Put the mustard seed mixture into a blender. Cover and process until of a spreading consistency, but still grainy.
3. Remove to a storage container. Stir in the horseradish, honey, and salt.

YIELD: About 2 cups.

Beverages

Mimosa

A brunch beverage that is an elegant way to start the meal.

> *Champagne*
> *Fresh orange juice*
> *Orange slice and mint sprig for garnish*

Fill a tall champagne glass three-quarters full with champagne. Top with fresh orange juice. Garnish with a slice of orange and a sprig of mint.

YIELD: 1 serving.

Sangria

This is a favorite beverage for a brunch; it is also good as a summer cooler.

1 bottle dry red wine
¼ cup brandy
½ cup fresh lemon juice
½ cup fresh orange juice
½ cup sugar
1 7-ounce bottle club soda
½ orange, sliced
1 apple, cored and cut into wedges
1 cup seedless green grapes
Ice

1. In a large pitcher, combine all the ingredients. Stir to mix well.
2. Pour over ice in tall stemmed glasses. Garnish each glass with some of the fruit.

YIELD: 8 servings.

Bloody Mary

A wonderful classic brunch beverage or light cocktail before dinner. Garnish with a dill pickle spear or a whole cooked shrimp on the rim of the glass.

6 ounces canned tomato juice
Dash of fresh lemon juice
Pinch of prepared horseradish
Dash of Worcestershire sauce
Dash of hot pepper sauce
Pinch of celery salt
Pinch of freshly ground black pepper
1 jigger vodka
Dill pickle spear or cooked shrimp for garnish

1. In a shaker, combine all the ingredients except the vodka, pickle spear, and shrimp.
2. Pour the vodka over ice in a glass and top with the tomato mixture.
3. Garnish with the pickle or shrimp.

YIELD: 1 serving.

Hot Buttered Cranberry Grog

When the cold winter winds blow, this is the beverage to serve before brunch or after skiing.

> *1 quart cranberry juice cocktail*
> *2 tablespoons brown sugar*
> *4 cinnamon sticks*
> *1 teaspoon whole allspice*
> *1 teaspoon whole cloves*
> *¹/₃ to ¹/₂ cup golden rum*
> *Butter*

1. In a saucepan, heat the juice and spices to boiling. Simmer, covered, for 15 minutes.
2. Add the rum and remove from the heat.
3. Strain the juice and serve in tall mugs. Garnish with a cinnamon stick and top with a pat of butter.

YIELD: 4 servings.

Café Brulôt

A perfect ending to a great meal or a wonderful evening at the theater.

> *1 cup brandy*
> *Peel of 1 orange*
> *4 whole cloves*
> *4 whole allspice*
> *2 cinnamon sticks*
> *¹/₄ cup sugar*
> *3 cups very strong, hot coffee*

1. In a saucepan, heat all the ingredients except the coffee until just hot.
2. Strain into a heat-resistant bowl. Ignite the brandy and allow to flame for 1 to 2 minutes.
3. Add the coffee to the brandy mixture and ladle into coffee cups.

YIELD: 4 servings.

Café au Lait

What a relaxing way to finish a great meal! Especially nice if you can serve this right at the table.

> *Brewed strong French-roast coffee*
> *Warm milk*

Pour equal amounts of brewed coffee and warmed milk into coffee cups at the same time. Serve immediately.

Irish Coffee

Specialty coffees are nice alternatives to a sweet dessert. Serve them in a stemmed coffee mug. Pass a plate of tiny tea cookies.

> *Heavy cream*
> *1 cup freshly brewed dark-roast coffee*
> *1 teaspoon sugar*
> *Irish whiskey to taste*
> *Pinch of ground cinnamon*
> *Pinch of cocoa powder*

1. Whip the cream until stiff peaks form.
2. Pour the coffee into a cup and stir in the sugar.
3. Add the Irish whiskey. Top with a dollop of cream and sprinkle with cinnamon and cocoa.

YIELD: 1 serving.

10
Desserts, Sweets, and Munchies

Yes, you can prepare desserts, sweets, and great snacks on *one burner*.

There are no-bake cookies, pies, delicious sauces for ice cream, baked apples, and cooked fruit sauces. There's even a skillet cake that you can bake. All the recipes are easy to prepare in a small cooking area, and all are foolproof! The simplicity of these desserts and snacks are in keeping with the entire mood of this book.

If you are, indeed, cooking on *one burner*, choose a dessert recipe that must be prepared ahead: Poached Pears in Cognac or Espresso Mousse are good examples. These time-saving recipes free the cook and the burner from last-minute preparation. If you want an elegant last-minute dessert, be sure it takes a different utensil from the one needed for your main dish. For an elegant but fast dessert, just serve a special ice cream sauce, such as Mocha-Fudge Sauce or Peach Melba Sundae. And for real fun, prepare one of the fondue recipes. They're perfect for a small relaxed party of 2 to 6 people.

Remember, the dessert is the finale to the meal. Make it memorable by an impeccable presentation. Brew a pot of coffee from the finest beans to serve with the pièce de résistance! *Bon Appétit!*

Hints for the Baked One-Burner Dessert (No Oven Required!)

Cooking on *one burner* is sometimes more challenging than having several burners and an oven at your disposal. There are many tips that can make this concept work for you.

Did you know that you can bake cakes on a single burner? Moist cakes and cakes that have "gooey" toppings, like an upside-down cake, can be successfully prepared. Even the fluted tube pans can be used provided you have a large Dutch oven that will accommodate the size of the pan.

1. *Bundt Cakes*—Prepare according to package or recipe directions, bake on a rack in a Dutch oven over medium-high heat.
2. *Upside-Down Cakes*—Follow the recipe on page 196 for specific directions.
3. *Moist Quick Breads and Brownies*—Moist nut breads, such as banana nut, can be prepared right in the skillet. Skillets with nonstick finishes are recommended. Spray with vegetable cooking spray. Pour the batter into the skillet, cover, and bake over very low heat. Be careful not to use recipes that have a high sugar content or chocolate bits in the batter. They tend to burn on the bottom. Check doneness with a toothpick. Let cool for 10 minutes and flip onto a rack to finish cooling. Cut into wedges to serve. See page 197 for specific directions.
4. *Custards*—Baked egg custards can be prepared in a skillet. See page 193 for specific instructions. Remember that the water should never boil or the custard will weep as it cools.

Sweet Gifts from Your Kitchen

There are times when a gift of food is just the perfect touch. With the many packaged foods available today, a homemade gift is especially appreciated.

Packaging your delicacy is always a challenge, but this step will be half the fun. Gingham bows, wicker baskets, and old-fashioned canning jars are a few ideas that can add the charming wrapper your creations deserve.

Once you have given several food gifts, you will begin to look for containers as you shop. A walk through the department stores will spark your imagination for the unusual. Any store can be a source for a memorable, yet practical, holder for your delicious gift. Even an antique market or rummage sale can inspire the creative shopper.

I tend to set a few containers aside, ready for that spur-of-the-moment gift; then, when the occasion arises, I simply go to my repertoire of gift-giving recipes and prepare one that's appropriate.

Always label the container with the name of the recipe and any directions for how to use or store the contents. If you desire, include the recipe on a pretty card for a special touch. You may want to keep a few of your recipes a secret or the entire neighborhood will prepare your exclusive delicacies.

Many of the recipes in this chapter are especially good for gift giving. Everyone loves sweets and munchies! Below is a list of the recipes and container suggestions to consider as gifts for your next occasion.

Chocolate-Caramel Rum Sauce

Peanut Butter Ice Cream Sauce

Mocha-Fudge Sauce

Eggnog Fondue

Chocolate Fondue

Fresh Fruit Compote

Poached Pears in Cognac

Marinated Melon

Skillet Fudge Cookies

Peanut Butter Chewies

Cashew Clusters

Snack and Mix

Spiced Nuts

Fudge Brownie Wedges

Turtle Candies

Chocolate Truffles

CONTAINER IDEAS

· Keep a variety of different-size plastic bags handy for popcorn and other food nibbles. Close with a ribbon. Or use large tin containers that are decorated with interesting nostalgic designs or bright colors.

· Many variety stores stock colorful cardboard containers that are inexpensive but attractive enough to hold your loving gift.

· Canning jars and replicas of antique storage containers are perfect for dessert sauces and fruit marinades. The covers can be decorated to add a creative touch.

- Candies and cookies can be packaged in elegant boxes available in stores that sell candy making supplies. Always line the box with greaseproof paper to prevent saturation. Add a stunning bow and you have an impressive gift.
- For housewarming gifts it is especially thoughtful to give a gift that is filled with a treat. In that way, the food can be enjoyed immediately and the container can serve to decorate the home for years to come.

Apples in Rum Custard Sauce

This autumn dessert is festive enough for company. Serve it in a stemmed glass for an elegant touch and pass a pretty pitcher of Rum Custard Sauce.

> *⅓ cup butter or margarine*
> *8 tart apples, peeled and sliced*
> *½ cup golden raisins*
> *½ teaspoon ground cinnamon*
> *¼ teaspoon ground nutmeg*
> *Pinch of ground cloves*
> *Rum Custard Sauce (following recipe)*

1. In a frying pan, melt the butter over medium heat. Add the apples, raisins, and seasonings. Cook the apples until they are soft but firm.
2. Serve warm with Rum Custard Sauce.

YIELD: 8 servings.

Rum Custard Sauce

> *6 large egg yolks*
> *1 cup heavy cream*
> *1 cup milk*
> *½ cup sugar*
> *2 tablespoons dark rum*
> *2 teaspoons vanilla extract*

1. In a saucepan, combine the egg yolks, cream, milk, and sugar. Cook over low heat until thickened, stirring constantly. Do not allow to boil.
2. Remove from the heat, stir in the rum and vanilla. Chill before serving.

YIELD: 2³/₄ cups.

Autumn Baked Apples

Enjoy the nostalgic flavor of baked apples, each served in its own cup, prepared in your skillet.

> *4 medium-size baking apples*
> *4 tablespoons brown sugar*
> *Ground cinnamon*
> *Heavy cream or plain yogurt*

1. Core the apples and put each in a custard cup.
2. Put 1 tablespoon of sugar and a pinch of cinnamon in the hollow of each apple.
3. Put the custard cups in a skillet. Add enough water to the skillet to reach halfway up each cup. Cover and cook over low heat until the apples are soft, about 15 to 20 minutes. Serve with cream or plain yogurt.

YIELD: 4 servings.

Bananas Flambé

For a finale with a flourish, try this flaming dessert, and listen for the oohs and ahs.

> *¹/₄ cup butter or margarine*
> *¹/₂ cup brown sugar*
> *¹/₄ cup raisins*
> *¹/₂ teaspoon vanilla extract*
> *Pinch of ground cloves*
> *Pinch of ground nutmeg*
> *Pinch of ground cinnamon (continued)*

> 4 ripe bananas, sliced
> 1/4 cup banana liqueur
> 1/2 cup 151 proof rum
> 1 pint French vanilla ice cream

1. In a frying pan, melt the butter over medium heat. Add the sugar, raisins, vanilla, and spices. Cook and stir until the sugar has dissolved.
2. Add the banana slices and heat through in the sugar mixture, turning the bananas several times to coat them.
3. Pour the liqueur and rum over the mixture in the pan and carefully ignite them with a long match. When the flames subside, ladle the bananas and sauce over individual portions of ice cream.

YIELD: 4 servings.

Cherries Jubilee

Perfect for the last-minute hostess. Flame this spectacular dessert right at the table with the lights turned down low.

> 2 16-ounce cans or jars pitted dark sweet cherries,
>   drained and 1 cup syrup reserved
> 1/4 cup currant jelly
> 1/4 cup fresh orange juice
> 1 cup reserved cherry syrup
> 2 tablespoons cornstarch
> 2 tablespoons butter or margarine
> 2 pints French vanilla ice cream
> 8 Basic Crêpes (page 21), optional
> 1/2 cup Cognac or brandy

1. In a saucepan, combine the jelly, orange juice, and 3/4 cup of the cherry syrup. Simmer until the jelly has dissolved.
2. Combine the remaining 1/4 cup cherry syrup and the cornstarch. Stir into the hot mixture and cook and stir until thickened. Add the cherries and butter and heat through.
3. Spoon the ice cream into serving dishes or into the center of the crêpes. Fold the sides of the crêpes over the ice cream.
4. Heat the Cognac and pour it over the cherries. Ignite with a long match.

5. When the flames have subsided, spoon the cherry sauce over the ice cream or filled crêpes and serve immediately.

YIELD: 4 to 8 servings.

NOTE: The crêpes may be filled several days ahead and frozen until serving time.

Poached Pears in Cognac

Poached pears are a perfect light ending to any meal.

> *8 medium-size firm ripe pears, peeled and*
> *   left whole with stems on*
> *1 cup sugar*
> *Peel of 1 orange*
> *1 cinnamon stick*
> *8 whole cloves*
> *½ cup Cognac*

1. Put the pears, sugar, orange peel, and spices in a saucepan or Dutch oven. Add enough water to cover the pears and bring the mixture to a boil. Cover and simmer until the pears are tender, about 20 minutes. Be careful not to overcook them.
2. Cool the pears in the poaching liquid. Then stir in the Cognac. Chill until ready to serve.
3. Top each pear with some Cognac sauce and serve.

YIELD: 8 servings.

Variation
    To make Poached Pears with Chocolate Sauce, prepare the pears as directed and chill. Before serving, prepare Mocha-Fudge Sauce (page 204) and drizzle the warm sauce over the drained pears.

Strawberries with Raspberry Purée

Garnish with a rich chocolate brownie for a glamorous dessert at any time of the year. The Raspberry Purée can also be served over fruit, cake, pancakes, or French toast.

*1 12-ounce package frozen raspberries (without syrup), or 3 cups
  fresh raspberries
2 tablespoons sugar
2 teaspoons cornstarch
¼ cup raspberry liqueur
2 pints fresh strawberries, hulled*

1. In a blender, purée the raspberries, sugar, and cornstarch until smooth.
2. In a saucepan, heat the raspberry mixture over medium-low heat until thickened and glossy. Remove from the heat and stir in the liqueur. Strain it through a sieve, if desired, then chill.
3. When ready to serve, spoon the raspberry purée over the strawberries in tall stemmed glasses.

YIELD: 4 servings.

Fruit Fritters

This dessert is guaranteed to be a favorite after dinner or after a fancy brunch. You could serve it as a main dish for brunch, just as you would serve pancakes or French toast. This recipe does require last-minute preparation, so plan accordingly.

*1 large egg
2 tablespoons granulated sugar
¼ cup fresh lemon juice
1 cup all-purpose flour
1 teaspoon baking powder
Pinch of salt
⅔ cup milk
Oil for deep-fat frying
4 oranges, peeled, seeded, and cut into thick slices, or 4 to 6
  bananas, cut into 1½-inch chunks
Confectioner's sugar*

1. In a mixing bowl, combine the egg and granulated sugar. Beat until light and thick. Add the lemon juice and mix well.
2. Sift together the flour, baking powder, and salt. Add to the egg mixture alternately with the milk, beating well after each addition.

3. In a skillet, heat a 1-inch depth of oil to 375 to 400 degrees.
4. Dip the fruit into the batter to coat it. Fry in the hot oil until puffed and golden, turning once. Drain on paper towels. Dust with confectioner's sugar and serve at once.

YIELD: 4 to 6 servings.

Fresh Fruit Compote

This refreshing light dessert can be prepared with any combination of your favorite seasonal fresh fruits. The compote improves with age, so prepare it several days ahead to allow the flavors to mellow.

1 large apple, cored and diced
4 ripe nectarines, pitted and sliced
1 16-ounce can pineapple chunks, packed in natural juices,
   drained and liquid reserved
1 cup seedless red or green grapes, halved
1½ cups fresh berries (strawberries, blueberries, or raspberries can
   all be used)
1 cup fresh orange juice
½ cup reserved pineapple juice
½ cup Sauternes
¼ cup sugar
1 cinnamon stick, optional

1. In a large bowl, combine the fruit.
2. In a saucepan, combine the remaining ingredients and bring to a boil. Pour the hot mixture over the fruit. Stir gently. Cover and chill for several hours. Before serving, remove the cinnamon stick.
3. Serve alone, garnished with a sprig of fresh mint, or as a sauce over ice cream or pound cake.

YIELD: 4 to 6 servings.

Marinated Melon

Summer is the time to enjoy the wonderful variety of fresh, sweet melons. This recipe combines all your favorites and allows their flavors to mingle for several hours. Substitute your favorite winter fruits in the fall.

> *¼ cup honey*
> *¼ cup water*
> *¼ cup fresh lime juice*
> *¼ cup Grand Marnier*
> *1 cup watermelon balls*
> *1 cup honeydew balls*
> *1 cup cantaloupe balls*
> *2 bananas, cut into chunks*

1. In a saucepan, combine the honey and water and bring to a boil. Lower the heat and simmer for 3 minutes.
2. Stir in the lime juice and liqueur and cool.
3. Put the melon balls in a large bowl and pour the honey mixture over them. Cover and refrigerate for several hours.
4. Just before serving, add the bananas and toss well.
5. Serve as a first course for a brunch or as a dessert for lunch or dinner.

YIELD: 6 to 8 servings.

Eggnog Fondue

This holiday treat takes no time at all to prepare. If you want to serve this dessert at other than holiday time, buy canned eggnog.

> *1 3-ounce package vanilla pudding mix (regular cooked pudding)*
> *1½ cups thick eggnog*
> *2 tablespoons golden rum*
> *Angel food or pound cake, cut into bite-size cubes*
> *Fresh fruit, cut into bite-size chunks*

1. In a saucepan or fondue pot, combine the pudding mix and eggnog. Cook over medium heat, stirring constantly, until thick. Stir in the rum.
2. Serve with cubed cake or fresh fruit sections as dippers.

YIELD: 4 servings.

NOTE: Leftover eggnog is excellent to use for French toast. Simply dip the bread into eggnog and fry on a greased hot griddle.

Chocolate Fondue

A dessert fondue is a delightful way to keep the party glowing throughout the evening. Serve with a variety of colorful fresh fruit dippers and squares of angel food or pound cake.

> *6 1-ounce squares unsweetened baking chocolate*
> *1½ cups sugar*
> *1 cup heavy cream*
> *½ cup butter or margarine*
> *¼ cup crème de cacao*
> *Assorted fruit and cake dippers, cut into 1½-inch cubes*

1. In a saucepan or fondue pot, combine the chocolate, sugar, cream, and butter. Cook over low heat, stirring frequently, until the mixture is smooth.
2. Add the crème de cacao and blend well.
3. Place the fondue pot in the center of your table. Give your guests fondue forks and let them use the assorted fruits and cake squares as dippers.

YIELD: 8 servings.

English Trifle

Traditionally, this recipe was a way to use leftover cake, jams, and fruits. Today, it's a combination of many wonderful ingredients layered decoratively in a clear glass bowl and left to mellow for 1 to 3 days in the refrigerator. Save this dessert for festive occasions when time runs out.

> *1 10- to 12-ounce pound cake*
> *1 10-ounce jar raspberry jam, with or without seeds*
> *½ cup dry sherry or Marsala*
> *1 16-ounce can sliced peaches, drained*
> *1 16-ounce can or jar pitted dark sweet cherries,*
> *   drained (continued)*

¼ cup plus 2 tablespoons sugar
2 tablespoons cornstarch
3 large egg yolks
3 cups milk
1 teaspoon vanilla extract
1 cup heavy cream
½ cup sliced almonds

1. Slice the cake into ⅜-inch-thick slices. Spread one side of each slice with jam.
2. Place a layer of cake (jam side up) in the bottom of a clear glass bowl. Sprinkle with a little sherry. Top with a layer of peaches and a few cherries. Repeat until all the cake, jam, wine, and fruit have been used.
3. In a saucepan, combine ¼ cup of the sugar, cornstarch, and egg yolks with a wire whisk. Add the milk in a slow steady stream, stirring with the whisk.
4. Cook over medium-low heat, stirring constantly, until thickened. Remove from the heat and cool to room temperature. Add the vanilla.
5. Pour the cooled pudding over the layered cake.
6. Whip the cream until soft peaks form. Add the remaining 2 tablespoons of sugar and continue to beat until stiff peaks form.
7. Spread or pipe the cream with a pastry tube over the trifle. Sprinkle with the sliced almonds. Cover the bowl with plastic wrap and refrigerate for up to 3 days.
8. To serve, spoon the trifle onto pretty dessert plates at the table or pass the entire bowl, allowing your guests to help themselves.

YIELD: 8 to 10 servings.

TIME-SAVING HINT: Prepare a large package of vanilla pudding and pie filling instead of preparing the cooked pudding above. Use 3 cups of the cooled pudding and proceed as directed above.

Zabaglione

A very elegant dessert that has many variations for real versatility. Serve it warm by itself or chilled over fresh berries. I especially like to serve it over fresh raspberries or sliced fresh peaches. If you want to serve it warm, this is a last-minute dessert, so plan accordingly.

> *4 large egg yolks*
> *1 large egg*
> *½ cup sugar*
> *⅓ cup Marsala*

1. Combine all the ingredients in the top of a double boiler. Cook over rapidly boiling water, beating constantly with an electric hand mixer or wire whisk. Beat until the mixture doubles and thickens.
2. Remove from the heat and continue to beat for 1 minute.
3. Serve warm in tall stemmed glasses or chilled as a topping over fresh berries.

YIELD: 6 servings.

Pumpkin Pudding with Brandy Cream

When the autumn winds begin to blow, thoughts of spicy pumpkin pie come to mind. Now you can have all the taste of this favorite without the work. Garnish with "spirited" whipped cream and serve with a delicious cup of rich gourmet coffee.

> *2 large eggs*
> *1 cup canned or freshly puréed pumpkin*
> *½ cup packed brown sugar*
> *¼ teaspoon salt*
> *1 teaspoon pumpkin pie spice*
> *¾ cup half-and-half*
> *½ cup heavy cream*
> *1 teaspoon brandy*
> *Pinch of ground cinnamon*

1. In a mixing bowl, combine the eggs, pumpkin, sugar, salt, pumpkin pie spice, and half-and-half. Mix well with a wire whisk.

2. Pour into four 6-ounce custard or soufflé cups.
3. Place the cups in a skillet and carefully pour in enough hot water between the cups to come halfway up the sides of the cups.
4. Cover and simmer until a knife inserted in the center of the custard comes out clean, about 25 minutes. Remove the cups from the water and cool to room temperature.
6. Before serving, whip the cream until soft peaks form. Add the brandy and whip until stiff.
7. Serve each pudding with a dollop of cream sprinkled with cinnamon.

YIELD: 4 servings.

NOTE: This recipe can easily be doubled if your skillet will hold 8 custard cups.

Butterscotch and Toffee Pudding

Homemade pudding is so easy and so good. Why not prepare it tonight?

> *¾ cup packed brown sugar*
> *2 tablespoons cornstarch*
> *¼ teaspoon salt*
> *2 cups milk*
> *1 large egg, well beaten*
> *3 tablespoons butter or margarine*
> *1 teaspoon vanilla extract*
> *Whipped cream*
> *1 chocolate-coated toffee candy bar, crushed*

1. In a saucepan, combine the sugar, cornstarch, salt, and milk. Mix well and cook over medium heat, stirring constantly, until thickened. Then cook 2 minutes longer.
2. Stir a small amount of the hot custard into the beaten egg; then add the egg mixture to the saucepan. Cook and stir for 2 minutes.
3. Remove the custard from the heat and stir in the butter and vanilla.
4. Pour the pudding into small serving cups. Cover and chill.

5. To serve, garnish each serving with a dollop of whipped cream and sprinkle with the crushed toffee.

YIELD: 4 servings.

Kahlua Custard

This recipe proves that you don't have to use an oven to bake egg custards, nor do you have to prepare enough to feed a crowd. You may, however, double this recipe, if desired.

> *2 large eggs, lightly beaten*
> *2 tablespoons sugar*
> *¹/₄ teaspoon salt*
> *1 cup milk, warmed*
> *2 tablespoons Kahlua*
> *Pinch of ground nutmeg*
> *Whipped cream*
> *Chocolate shavings*

1. Combine the first 5 ingredients in a bowl and pour into 2 or 3 custard or individual soufflé cups. Sprinkle with nutmeg.
2. Place the cups on a rack in a skillet containing water just under the boiling point. The water should reach the middle of the cups.
3. Cover and simmer over low heat until the custards are firm, about 10 to 12 minutes. Do not allow the water to boil. Cover and chill the custards for several hours before serving.
4. To serve, garnish with whipped cream and chocolate shavings.

YIELD: 2 to 3 servings.

Espresso Mousse

This recipe's a dream to prepare!

> *1½ cups very strong coffee*
> *48 large marshmallows*
> *1 cup heavy cream, whipped*
> *Whipped cream and grated chocolate for garnish, optional*

1. In a large saucepan, heat the coffee and marshmallows over medium heat. Stir and cook until smooth. Then chill until slightly thickened.
2. Fold in the whipped cream and chill until ready to serve.
3. Spoon into stemmed dessert glasses. Garnish with additional whipped cream and grated chocolate, if desired.

YIELD: 4 to 6 servings.

Mandarin Chocolate Mousse

Chocolate-lovers, take note! This recipe combines the delightful flavors of chocolate and orange. Serve this extra-rich dessert in small chocolate or soufflé cups.

> *4 1-ounce squares semisweet chocolate*
> *⅓ cup fresh orange juice*
> *Pinch of salt*
> *3 large eggs, separated*
> *1 teaspoon vanilla extract*
> *Canned or fresh mandarin orange sections*

1. In a saucepan, combine the chocolate, orange juice, and salt. Cook over low heat until smooth. Remove from the heat and quickly stir in the egg yolks and vanilla. Cool.
2. Beat the egg whites until stiff but not dry. Fold into the chocolate mixture.
3. Pour into small chocolate cups or soufflé dishes and garnish with the orange sections. Chill for at least 1 hour before serving.

YIELD: 4 to 6 servings.

Peach Melba Sundae

This is a simple but pretty dessert that is served in many elegant restaurants around the world. Save it for the hectic days, because the sauce must be prepared ahead of time and chilled.

¼ cup currant jelly
3 cups fresh or frozen raspberries
2 tablespoons cornstarch
1 tablespoon raspberry liqueur
1 pint French vanilla ice cream
1 16-ounce can peach slices, drained

1. In a saucepan, combine the jelly and raspberries. Cook over low heat until the jelly melts.
2. Combine the cornstarch and liqueur and stir the mixture into the berries. Cook and stir over medium heat until slightly thickened.
2. If desired, strain the sauce through a sieve to remove the seeds. Cover and chill.
3. Serve the raspberry sauce over the ice cream and sliced peaches in sherbet or parfait glasses.

YIELD: 6 to 8 servings.

Candy Bar Pie

Here's a chocolate-lover's delight!

40 large marshmallows
½ cup milk
1 8-ounce milk chocolate bar with whole almonds
1 pint heavy cream, whipped
1 prepared 8- or 9-inch graham cracker or chocolate cookie crumb crust
Whipped cream for garnish, optional

1. In a saucepan, combine the marshmallows, milk, and chocolate. Cook over low heat, stirring constantly, until the mixture is smooth. Cool until thickened.
2. Fold in the whipped cream and pour into the prepared crust.

Cover and chill for several hours. Serve with additional whipped cream, if desired.

YIELD: 6 to 8 servings.

Caramel-Peach Upside-Down Cake

This is a delightful top-of-the-stove dessert, perfect for those who don't have an oven or for those who don't wish to heat up the kitchen. Serve it warm or at room temperature as a dessert or brunch cake.

> *3 tablespoons butter or margarine, melted*
> *½ cup packed brown sugar*
> *¼ cup sliced almonds*
> *¼ cup flaked coconut*
> *1 8-ounce can peach slices, drained*
> *4 large eggs, separated*
> *1 cup granulated sugar*
> *1 cup all-purpose flour*
> *1 teaspoon baking powder*
> *Whipped cream for garnish*

1. In a 9- or 10-inch skillet, combine the butter, brown sugar, almonds, and coconut. Spread evenly over the bottom of the skillet.
2. Arrange the peach slices in a spiral pattern over the top of the sugar mixture.
3. Beat the egg yolks and granulated sugar until light. Combine the flour and baking powder and gradually add to the egg mixture. Mix well.
4. In a separate bowl, beat the egg whites until stiff. Carefully fold the beaten egg whites into the yolk mixture. Carefully pour the batter over the peaches.
5. Cover and bake over low heat for 20-25 minutes. When done, the cake will spring back when touched with a fingertip.
6. Put a large plate or platter over the skillet. Carefully invert the plate and skillet to turn the cake out onto the plate. Serve warm or at room temperature, garnished with whipped cream.

YIELD: 6 servings.

TIME-SAVING HINT: Prepare a one-layer yellow or white cake mix according to package directions instead of preparing the cake from scratch. Proceed as above.

Fudge Brownie Wedges

If you like chewy, rich chocolate brownies, this is the recipe for you. Serve it by itself with a garnish of confectioner's sugar, or top it with your favorite ice cream and freeze until firm. Now you have a dessert that's ready to serve at a moment's notice. I like to add the Mocha-Fudge Sauce as a special finishing touch. Heavenly and very pretty! *(Bake these in a heavy-gauge aluminum skillet only.)*

> *2 1-ounce squares unsweetened baking chocolate*
> *½ cup butter or margarine*
> *2 large eggs*
> *1 cup sugar*
> *1 teaspoon vanilla extract*
> *½ cup all-purpose flour*
> *1 cup chopped walnuts*
>
> *Confectioner's sugar*
> *1 pint ice cream, flavor of your choice*
> *Mocha-Fudge Sauce (page 204)*

1. In a small saucepan, melt the chocolate and butter. Remove from the heat and cool to room temperature.
2. In a mixing bowl, beat the eggs. Add the sugar, vanilla, and cooled chocolate mixture. Mix well.
3. Stir in the flour and walnuts and mix until moistened.
4. Pour the batter into a greased 9- or 10-inch skillet. Cover and cook over very low heat for 20 to 30 minutes. The brownie will pull away from the sides of the skillet when done.
5. Put the skillet on a wire rack and cool for 20 minutes. To remove the brownie, place the cooling rack over the skillet and turn over. Cool to room temperature.

6. Sprinkle with confectioner's sugar or top with your favorite ice cream that has been softened slightly. Then freeze until firm.
7. Cut the brownie into wedges and serve with warm Mocha-Fudge Sauce.

YIELD: 8 servings.

SERVING SUGGESTIONS

Peppermint Pie—Top the brownie with pink peppermint ice cream. Garnish with whole peppermint candies.

Mandarin Chocolate Pie—Top the brownie with orange sherbet. Garnish with mandarin orange sections.

Mint-Chip Pie—Top the brownie with green mint ice cream with chocolate chips. Garnish each serving with chocolate-covered after-dinner mints.

Lacy Brownie Wedges—Place a paper doily on the plain brownie before sprinkling with confectioner's sugar. Remove the doily to expose the lacy design. Cut into wedges.

Skillet Fudge Cookies

Now you can prepare rich fudge cookies without turning on the oven.

> *1½ cups sliced almonds*
> *2 1-ounce squares unsweetened chocolate*
> *1 14-ounce can sweetened condensed*
> * milk*
> *2½ cups vanilla wafer crumbs*

1. Sprinkle ¼ cup of the almonds over the bottom of a greased 9-inch square baking pan.
2. In a saucepan, heat the chocolate and milk over low heat. Cook and stir until the mixture is thick, about 10 minutes.

3. Remove from the heat, stir in the crumbs. Spread over the nuts in the pan. Top with the remaining almonds. Cover the top of the mixture with plastic wrap and pat the top smooth.
4. Chill for several hours. Cut into squares to serve.

YIELD: 25 cookies.

Peanut Butter Chewies

If you like peanut butter and want a quick snack for kids and adults alike, here's the cookie for you! This recipe invites child participation.

> *½ cup sugar*
> *½ teaspoon salt*
> *¾ cup light corn syrup*
> *1 cup creamy peanut butter*
> *1 cup chopped roasted peanuts*
> *6 cups corn flakes*

1. In a saucepan, combine the sugar, salt, and corn syrup. Cook over medium heat until the sugar is dissolved. Blend in the peanut butter and remove from the heat.
2. Put the nuts and corn flakes into a large mixing bowl and pour the hot syrup over them. Toss to coat well.
3. Drop by tablespoonfuls onto wax paper. Cool, then store in an airtight container.

YIELD: 3 to 4 dozen.

Cashew Clusters

This no-bake cookie is a tradition, but this version has a more sophisticated touch with the addition of the roasted cashews. Add your own personal touch with your favorite roasted nuts or even raisins.

> *1 6-ounce package butterscotch bits*
> *1 6-ounce package semisweet chocolate bits*
> *1 3-ounce can chow mein noodles*
> *1 cup salted cashews*

1. In a saucepan, melt the butterscotch and chocolate bits over low heat.
2. Remove from the heat and fold in the remaining ingredients.
3. Drop by teaspoonfuls onto wax paper. Chill until set.

YIELD: 4 dozen.

Chocolate Truffles

If you like chocolate, this will make the perfect ending to a meal for you. These little candies are very rich, very elegant, and very easy to prepare. Serve them with a pot of piping hot, freshly brewed coffee or give them as a gift from your kitchen.

> *¼ cup heavy cream*
> *2 tablespoons Amaretto*
> *8 ounces semisweet chocolate bits*
> *¼ cup butter or margarine*
> *Gourmet baking cocoa, chopped nuts, or chocolate sprinkles*

1. In a saucepan, boil the cream until it is reduced by half. Remove from the heat.
2. Stir in the Amaretto and chocolate bits. Return to low heat and stir until melted.
3. Add the butter and refrigerate the mixture until firm, about 30 minutes.
4. Shape into 1-inch balls. Roll in cocoa, chopped nuts, or chocolate shot. Cover and refrigerate until ready to serve.

YIELD: 2 dozen.

Turtle Candies

Prepare your own delicious candies at home. These are also perfect to give as a gift from your kitchen.

> *1 cup large whole pecan halves*
> *½ pound caramels*
> *2 teaspoons heavy cream*
> *6-ounce package of semisweet chocolate chips*

1. On a greased baking sheet, make clusters of 4 pecan halves.
2. In a saucepan, melt the caramels with the cream over very low heat, stirring constantly until smooth.
3. Spoon the caramel mixture over the pecans, leaving the tips of the pecans exposed. Let set for 20 minutes, or until firm.
4. Meanwhile, melt the chocolate over very low heat. Let cool until thickened but still fluid.
5. Spread a small amount of chocolate over the caramel-pecan clusters. Allow to set. Cover and refrigerate.

YIELD: 24 candies.

NOTE: Substitute white confectionary coating (white chocolate) for the semisweet chocolate for a change from the traditional candy.

Snack and Mix

This combination of "goodies" is guaranteed to be the hit at your next informal party or as a TV treat during a football game.

> *⅓ cup butter or margarine*
> *1 tablespoon Worcestershire sauce*
> *½ teaspoon garlic powder*
> *½ teaspoon seasoned salt*
> *2 quarts popped corn*
> *2 cups pretzel sticks*
> *2 cups cheese curls*

1. In a Dutch oven, melt the butter over medium heat. Add the seasonings and mix well.
2. Add the remaining ingredients to the butter mixture and toss well. Turn the heat to low and toast the mixture for 10 minutes, stirring frequently. Cool in a large bowl.

YIELD: 3 quarts.

Spiced Nuts

This unusual snack makes an excellent hostess gift as well as a tasty appetizer served in your prettiest nut dish.

> *1 large egg white, beaten until frothy*
> *1 tablespoon water*
> *1/2 cup sugar*
> *1 teaspoon ground cinnamon*
> *1/2 teaspoon salt*
> *1/4 teaspoon ground nutmeg*
> *Pinch of ground cloves*
> *3 cups pecan halves*

1. In a skillet, combine the egg white, water, and sugar. Cook over medium heat until the mixture bubbles.
2. Add the spices and stir well. Add the nuts and stir and cook until the mixture coats the nuts and takes on a dry appearance.
3. Cool on wax paper. Store in an airtight container.

YIELD: 3 cups.

NOTE: Any variety of nut meats can be used.

Chocolate Whipped Cream

This is a wonderful recipe to keep in mind when you need a glamorous dessert topping. Use it to add a special touch to puddings and cakes or double the recipe and spread it as a frosting.

> *1/2 cup heavy cream*
> *1/2 square semisweet chocolate*

1. In a small saucepan, combine the cream and chocolate. Stir over very low heat until the chocolate has melted.
2. Remove from the heat and stir until the mixture is smooth. Cover and chill.
3. Just before serving, whip the cream until stiff.
4. Serve as a garnish or double the recipe and use it as a frosting. (Keep refrigerated.)

YIELD: 1 cup.

Peanut Butter Ice Cream Sauce

What a great way to turn vanilla or chocolate ice cream into a special dessert! Kids of all ages will love this one.

1 14-ounce can sweetened condensed milk
⅓ cup creamy peanut butter
¼ cup chopped salted cocktail peanuts

1. In a saucepan, heat all the ingredients over low heat.
2. Serve warm over ice cream. Garnish with additional chopped nuts.

YIELD: 1½ cups.

Chocolate-Caramel Rum Sauce

There's no need to spend hours preparing fancy desserts. By combining three ordinary ingredients, you will create a delightful ice cream dessert topping. The most challenging part of this recipe is making sure all the caramels make it to the saucepan!

6 to 8 ounces chocolate-covered caramels
2 tablespoons milk
2 tablespoons dark rum

1. In a saucepan, melt the candy with the milk over low heat. Stir in the rum.
2. Serve warm over French vanilla or coffee-flavored ice cream, garnished with roasted pecans or cashews.

YIELD: 4 servings.

Mocha-Fudge Sauce

This recipe can be prepared at a moment's notice. Just keep the ingredients on hand and you'll be ready to add a homemade touch to ice cream and cake desserts.

> *1 1-ounce square unsweetened chocolate*
> *¼ cup confectioner's sugar*
> *¼ cup milk*
> *1 teaspoon instant coffee granules*

1. In a saucepan, melt the chocolate, sugar, milk, and coffee granules over low heat. Stir constantly until thickened and smooth.
2. Serve warm over your favorite ice cream or cake.

YIELD: 2 servings.

NOTE: The recipe may be doubled or tripled as needed.

Glossary of Cooking Terms

If you're a novice cook, the language of the kitchen can be foreign enough to make you want to continue going out for fast foods. This section will give you a quick reference to those mysterious words used in this book and other basic cookbooks.

Al dente—Cooking pasta so that it's done but firm.

Baste—To moisten foods by brushing with melted butter, pan drippings, marinades, or other liquids.

Beat—A rapid movement to combine ingredients using a fork, spoon, wire whisk, or electric mixer.

Blend—To combine ingredients until just mixed.

Boil—To heat liquids until bubbles form that cannot be "stirred down." In the case of water, the temperature will reach 212 degrees.

Bone—To remove meat from the bone before cooking.

Braise—To cook slowly in a small amount of liquid, generally to tenderize less tender cuts of meat.

Bread—To coat foods with fine bread or cracker crumbs. Foods are dipped in a liquid to moisten and then in crumbs before frying. (It's a good idea to bread meat, fowl, or fish about 30 minutes before frying, because the breading adheres better if you do.)

Brown—To cook foods in a small amount of fat over medium to high heat until the foods become brown in color.

Chop—To cut foods into small pieces of ¼ to ¾ inch, depending on the type of food processed.

Cream—To beat ingredients together to a smooth consistency, usually in the case of butter and sugar for baking.

Cube—To cut into very uniform ½- to 1-inch square pieces.

Dash—A very small amount, less than ⅛ teaspoon. If using a shaker, a dash would comprise a quick flip of the container.

Deep-fry—To cook in enough hot oil or fat to completely cover foods while cooking. Oil temperatures usually range from 360 to 400 degrees.

Dice—To cut into small cubes about ⅛ to ¼ inch square.

Dissolve—To blend a dry ingredient into a liquid until smooth and no longer visible.

Drain—To remove liquid from a mixture, usually with the use of a colander or sieve.

Dredge—To coat foods with flour or other dry ingredients. Most often done to a roast or stew meat before browning.

Drop—To place by spoonfuls on a flat surface or into a hot mixture, such as dumplings dropped in stew or cookie batter dropped on a pan.

Fold—To incorporate several ingredients by careful and gentle turning with a spatula. Used generally when combining beaten egg whites into other ingredients.

Fry—To cook in a shallow pan with a small amount of fat over medium or high heat.

Garnish—To decorate a dish just before serving to make it more eye appealing. Simple garnishes include edible fresh fruits and vegetables that add color contrast to the plate.

Grate—To shred finely by using a mechanical or electric grater. Parmesan cheese and citrus rind are typical grated foods.

Grease—To coat a pan or baking sheet with fat or oil to prevent food from sticking during cooking.

Julienne—To cut foods into long, thin shapes. Used for salads most often, such as chef's salad for the cooked ham, turkey, and cheese.

Marinate—To allow foods to rest in a seasoned liquid, called a marinade, for the purpose of tenderizing and adding flavor. Usually the marinade includes oil, wine or vinegar, and a variety of seasonings.

Matchstick—To cut meats (raw or cooked) and vegetables into very long and thin strips that resemble wooden matches, a popular cut for Chinese cookery and for sautéed vegetables. Similar to **Julienne**, except it is a finer cut.

Mince—To cut into very fine pieces.

Parboil—To cook partially, usually used in the case of vegetables and some meats.

Purée—To process foods to a smooth mixture. Used for baby foods, fruit, and vegetable sauces. Can be processed in a blender, food mill, food processor, or sieve.

Reduce—To boil liquids in a shallow pan for the purpose of evaporating and, consequently, thickening the mixture.

Sauté—To fry quickly in a small amount of fat, stirring constantly. Most often it's done with onions, mushrooms, and other chopped vegetables.

Sift—To process dry ingredients, such as flour, sugar, and leavening agents through a sieve for the purposes of removing lumps, adding air, and combining ingredients.

Simmer—To boil lightly over very low heat. Small bubbles should form around the edge of the pan, but there should not be large rolling bubbles as in a full rolling boil.

Steam—To cook meat, fish, vegetables, and fruit above boiling or simmering water. Food is placed on a rack or basket with small holes or slits in bottom, set above the water, covered, and cooked by the rising steam.

Stir-fry—To cook, with constant motion, finely cut meats and vegetables in a small amount of oil over high heat.

Whip—To beat quickly for the purpose of adding air and combining ingredients. Most often used with egg whites or heavy cream and processed with an electric mixer or wire whisk.

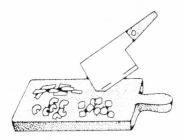

Substitutions

There are times when we all find that we're missing ingredients while in the midst of preparation. Well, all is not lost; there are substitutions that will save you a trip to the store at a most inconvenient time.

Baking Powder: 1 teaspoon—1 teaspoon cream of tartar plus ¼ teaspoon baking soda

Broth: 1 cup—1 teaspoon instant bouillon granules and 1 cup water

Buttermilk: 1 cup—1 tablespoon lemon juice or vinegar plus milk to equal 1 cup

Chocolate: 1 ounce unsweetened—3 tablespoons unsweetened cocoa plus 1 tablespoon butter or margarine

Cornstarch: 1 tablespoon—2 tablespoons flour or 4 teaspoons quick-cooking tapioca

Cream: 1 cup heavy—2 cups whipped dessert topping

1 Egg: whole—2 egg yolks

Garlic: 1 clove—⅛ teaspoon garlic powder

Herbs: 1 tablespoon snipped fresh—1½ teaspoons dried

Lemon: juice of 1 fresh—2 to 3 tablespoons bottled juice

Milk: 1 cup—4 tablespoons dry plus 1 cup water, or ½ cup evaporated milk plus ½ cup water

Mustard: 1 tablespoon—1 teaspoon powdered

Onion: 1 small—1 tablespoon minced instant onion

Tomato Sauce: 2 cups—¾ cup tomato paste plus 1 cup water

Yogurt: 1 cup—1 cup buttermilk

Index

A

Accompaniments:
 to the meal, 6
 to the sandwich, 33
Advance preparation, 7
Appetizers:
 chicken wings, 163
 chili con queso, 163
 eggplant strips, french fried,
  165
 fondue: quick cheese, 68; classic cheese, 139
 meat balls, Swedish, 104
 mushrooms, marinated, 164
 nuts, spiced, 202
 saganaki, 164
 shrimp bites, Dijon, 162
 snack and mix, 201
Apples. *See* Desserts
Apricots. *See* Desserts
Artichokes. *See* Chicken; Seafood

B

Bananas. *See* Desserts
Beans, lentils, peas (legumes):
 bean soup, hearty German, 99
 cassoulet, 61
 chili-bean franks, 71

lentil soup, 78
lots o'chili, 108
minestrone, new wave, 77
peasant beans and pasta, 118
pea soup with egg drop dumplings, bacon and, 100
Beef:
 burgers: B-L-T, 39; Florentine,
  39; gourmet, 38; Greek, 39;
  Italiano, 39; olé, 39; peppercorn, 39
 cabbage leaves, stuffed, 82
 chili: lots o', 108; mac, 60;
  Texas no-bean, 109
 Chimichangas, 58
 cream dried, 115
 eggplant skillet dinner, 107
 grab-a-mug meal, 59
 green peppers, stuffed, 105
 Hungarian goulash, 110
 Indonesian beef in pita bread,
  37
 liver sauté with bacon and
  herbs, 117
 marinated Korean, 150
 meat balls, Swedish, 104
 meat loaves with pesto sauce,
  106
 Mexi-joes, 37
 Mongolian, 150